MOSCOW

169 COLOUR ILLUSTRATIONS

BONECHI WB

CONTENTS

Revised and enlarged edition

Project and editorial conception: Casa Editrice Bonechi
Editorial director: Monica Bonechi
Picture research and graphic realization: Maria Katkova, Natalia Belyaeva
Cover: Sonia Gottardo
Editing: Sonia Gottardo

Text: Valeriy Evseev, Juriy Shabanov
Translation: Mikhail Nikolskiy, Victor Morgunov

© Copyright by CASA EDITRICE BONECHI
Via Cairoli 18b - 50131 Florence - Italy
Tel. 055 576841 - Fax 055 5000766 - E-mail: bonechi@bonechi.it - Internet: www.bonechi.it

Printed in Italy by Centro Stampa Editoriale Bonechi

Photos by: Vladimir Tikhomirov, Evgeniy German, Oleg Listopadov, Juriy Bykovskiy, Alexander Zakharchenko *and also from the photograph collections of* Welcome Books *and* Bonechi *Publishing Houses.*

ISBN 88-8029-809-7

* * *

A WORD ABOUT MOSCOW

Upon entering the Kremlin grounds through the arch of the Borovitsky Gate in the midst of the mighty walls of the Kremlin, a flood of dazzling yet gentle light envelops the visitor. Solemnly set back from the steep slope clothed in a festive froth of verdure are the Grand Kremlin Palace and the Armoury. The clean line of the walls is rhythmically broken by the verticals of ridge-roofed towers. Down below, beyond the brown-gray mirror of the granite-clad Moskva River, is the boundless expanse of the city enveloped in the haze of early spring warmth, with the light flourish of its skyline on the horizon, and the innumerable rows of houses vanishing in the distance, punctuated here and there by the solitary flash of a gilt church dome. With every gust of the impatient wind, the breath of the city arrives in a never-ceasing tide. A vast city. An old city. A lively city...

The history of Moscow and the Kremlin consists of an endless chain of events that go even further back into the hoary past than the eight and a half centuries that are documented in the chronicles. Prince Yuri, or Georgi, one of the younger children of the powerful Vladimir Monomachus, was nicknamed Dolgoruky (Long-Armed) for his indefatigable temperament, his quests for new possessions and his dream of the throne of a Grand Prince. In 1147, as is noted in the Ipatyevskaya Chronicle, he invited one of his princely allies to a meeting in Moscow. This was the first written mention of the city on which an estimate of its age can be based. In 1155, 65-year-old Yuri Dolgoruky ascended the throne in Kiev and a year later he "caused the city of Moscow to be built" at the mouth of the Neglinnaya River not far upstream from the mouth of another, navigable river, the Yauza.

That he "caused the city of Moscow to be built" does not, however, mean that it was built on virgin land. It simply refers to the construction of a new fortress to protect the old settlement on that part of Borovitsky Hill where the Armoury and the Palace of Congresses are located today. One of the oldest Slavic cultures, dating to the middle of the 1st millennium B.C., takes its name, Dyakovo, from the village near Kolomenskoye, once in the suburbs of Moscow, where archeologists uncovered the remains of an ancient settlement. Not long ago, potsherds of precisely the same type were unearthed during excavations on Kremlin Hill. As a result the real age of Moscow can be given as about twenty-five hundred years rather than eight and a half centuries.

The site offered various vantages as compared with other fortified towns in Northeastern Rus, and the importance of Moscow in the life of the Slavic lands grew as time wore on. It was situated at the intersection of trade routes which played an ever greater role in the economic life of the Slavs, from Rostov-the-Great, a town closely linked to the West, to the lands of Ryazan, and from Polotsk and Smolensk, which maintained contacts with Poland and Lithuania, to the Rostov Principality. Moscow easily established relations both with faraway Pomorye in the north and with Genoese colonies on the Black Sea. In general, one can hardly speak of isolation from Western Europe, for Yuri Dolgoruky himself counted Elizabeth, Queen of Norway, Anna, the wife of Henry I of France, and Anastasia, Queen of Hungary among his grandfather's sisters.

Life in Moscow was in many ways similar to life in the medieval cities of Western Europe and the cultural level was the same. In the Muscovites' everyday life, literacy and books and legal documents and, even, the game of draughts were as widespread as they were elsewhere. Even before Prince Yuri Dolgoruky began building the defences, Moscow had fortifications — a 700-metre-long stockade built along the crest of a low vallum, which was in turn surrounded by a wide moat. After its renovation, the area of the "city" increased markedly. The length of the walls now reached 1,200 metres. Built to form a triangle, they were additionally fortified with a 5-metre-deep moat whose width ranged between 12 and 14 metres.

"Hitzelin made me" reads the Latin inscription on the sword recently found during excavations in Ivan the Great Square in the Kremlin at the bottom of a moat which was once here. This sword is now the oldest specimen of side arms in the collection of the Kremlin museums. Weapons made by Hitzelin, a craftsman who supposedly worked in the Rhineland in 1130-1170, were famous all over Europe. Russian warriors both knew about the existence of these arms and had an opportunity to buy them, for the ties between the land of Moscow and Western Europe were quite active.

It took Moscow a hundred years after the reign of Prince Yuri Dolgoruky to acquire its own prince. Under Alexander Nevsky's will, his youngest son, Daniil, became the first Prince of Moscow. Early in the 13th century, the notion "Muscovites" became generally recognised and quite customary.

At the time, trade and crafts were developing in Moscow at a particularly brisk pace. Other lands began to gravitate towards the city, all the more so as it was situated in the centre of the territories of the Old Slavic tribes which, together with the Novgorod Slavs, constituted the nucleus of what was to become the Great Russian nation.

...Today this charred log house reassembled in the underground part of the Annunciation Cathedral is just a museum exhibit, the largest of those that date to the 13th century. An ordinary dwelling house which somehow miraculously survived a fire, it has preserved for posterity a terrible story of those distant years: a raid by nomads and a city fire. The hard times of the Tatar-Mongol invasion have left a thick layer of coals and ashes on Borovitsky Hill, eloquent evidence of a catastrophic fire. Djuveini, a Persian contemporary, had this to say about the devastation of Moscow by Khan Batu's hordes in 1238: "They left nothing but the name of the city behind them". How viable Moscow was and how great its economic potentials were become evident from the fact that, all the calamities notwithstanding, not only did it not decrease in size, but began outright to grow. Settlers from frontier principalities, which were most subject to nomad raids, willingly moved here. It was during this period, one of the most difficult in Russian history, that the Muscovites for the first time began using a new building material, stone, whereas formerly they had used only wood.

The first stone structures were built in Moscow under Prince Daniil Alexandrovich, the first Moscow prince, who thus marked the transformation of Moscow into an independent principality. His name has been preserved to this day in the names of a number of Moscow streets, and the St. Daniel Monastery, dedicated to his heavenly namesake and patron, St. Daniel Stylite, which he originally founded and which has now been returned to the Russian Orthodox Church, also reminds us of him. There is a supposition that it was within the walls of this monastery that Prince Daniil laid the cornerstone of Moscow's first stone church in 1272.

Prince Daniil's son, Ivan Danilovich, nicknamed Kalita (Moneybag) by his contemporaries for his tendency to hoarding, went down in history as the "gatherer of the Russian lands", and applied himself to the task of winning the title of Grand Prince. No sooner had he obtained this title, than he used all his new-won powers to make Moscow stronger, for he continued to consider the lands of Moscow and of Vladimir the centre of his possessions. Subsequently Grand Prince Ivan Danilovich won a victory which was quite remarkable for the Middle Ages: he prevailed on Metropolitan Pyotr to move his see from Tver to Moscow, which in effect confirmed the dominance of the Moscow Grand Prince over all the liege princes.

As a commemoration of all his victories, a number of stone churches, including the Metropolitan's Cathedral of the Dormition (1326) and the Grand Prince's Archangel Cathedral (1333), were built in the Kremlin. And in 1339-1340, new walls of oak were erected round the Kremlin on the orders of Ivan Kalita. This was a highly sophisticated fortification structure, which only stood for 15 years for another fire broke out in 1365, a particular-

ly dry year, and razed the Kremlin to the ground. On ascending the throne, Grand Prince Dmitri Donskoi, Ivan Kalita's grandson, decided to build a new fortress of white stone.

Thus Moscow was surrounded by a ring of new stone walls more than 60 metres outside the old ones, for it was necessary to ensure the protection of the **posad** (settlement), which had grown in size. In the course of restoration work carried out in the 1930s, small fragments of old masonry were uncovered. Judging from them, the 14th-century walls were 2 to 3 metres thick. The rate of construction work was amazing: the fortress was built within the space of one year. What mattered even more, however, was the fact that this was the first time ever that a stone fortress was built on the Vladimir-Suzdal lands. Formerly, only the inhabitants of Pskov and Novgorod-the-Great had erected stone fortifications. Both the process of construction and the material were quite new to the Muscovites. Stone quarries were opened near the village of Myachkovo 30 kilometres from Moscow, downstream on the Moskva River and it was thanks to this stone that Moscow began to be called a white-stone city.

To Dmitri Donskoi, the Kremlin was not only a formidable fortress. It was also a manifestation of the growing might of Moscow, which was now capable of reuniting the isolated forces of separate principalities into a single whole. The power of Moscow became a guarantee of the possibility itself of resisting the Horde and of liberating the entire Russian land from its yoke.

An army of an unprecedented size — 150,000 Russian warriors — was gathered at Kolomna and placed under the command of the Grand Prince of Moscow. In just one day a total of 200,000 men under arms were lost by both sides in the Battle of Kulikovo Field — a tremendous battle fought in the valley of the Don, the Nepryadva and the Krasivaya Mecha. It took the Russians seven days to bury all those who had fallen, and the days is still commemorated by the people. Every autumn, on Dmitri's Saturday, a celebration in memory of the fallen heroes of the Battle of Kulikovo is observed. In Moscow various places still exist which recall the rout of Khan Mamai, places which are dear to the heart of every Muscovite.

Solyanka Street was the road along which the Moscow detachments marched to Kulikovo Field and along which they returned after they had won the battle. The Church of All Saints on Kulishki, now Nogin Square, was founded by Dmitri Donskoi in 1380 to commemorate the victory. Since then the church has been rebuilt many times, yet fragments of the masonry of the original church have survived in its foundations. Another monument founded that same year is the Vysoko-Petrovsky Monastery in what is now Petrovka Street; it was a particular favourite of the Grand Prince of Moscow. In 1386, another cloister, the Rozhdestvensky (Nativity) Convent, founded by the mother of Vladimir Khrabry, a hero of the Battle of Kulikovo, was built in commemoration of the event. The street takes its name from this convent where the bereaved mothers and widows of the fallen participants of the Mamai slaughter found shelter. In 1393, Princess Yevdokia, the widow of Dmitri Donskoi, who had died an early death, ordered a white-stone Church of St. Lazarus to be built in the Kremlin in place of an older wooden structure. Later on, it was renamed the Church of the Nativity of Our Lord. Today this church, which was eventually incorporated

Red Square in the mid-19th century. Lithograph

into the walls of the palatial Church of the Nativity is the only one among the Kremlin structures that provides an idea of 14th-century Russian architecture.

The victory on Kulikovo Field brought in its wake a feeling of national unity and gave rise to national consciousness, which provided an impetus for the rapid development of culture. Moscow chronicles began to be written and such epic literary works as **The Tale of the Mamai Slaughter and Zadonshchina** appeared. By the end of the 14th century, Moscow had developed into the biggest Russian centre of trade and crafts with a rich **torg** (marketplace) and a rapidly growing **posad**. Moscow's external ties grew ever more active. The city continued to stand terrible sieges and in 1408 a great army led by Khan Yedigei approached the Kremlin wall, yet this could not set back the city's development: thus, in 1404 the first city clock was built in Moscow. In 1439, Moscow repulsed an attack by Khan Ulu Muhammed, who was dealt a crushing blow by the Russian warriors led by Boyar Vladimir Khovrin on the site of today's Arbat Square. Almost simultaneously, representatives of the Moscow state flatly rejected the decision of the Council of Florence on the union of the Catholic and Orthodox Churches under the authority of the Holy See. After the fall of Constantinople, captured by the Ottoman Turks in 1453, Moscow was given the title of Third Rome, the successor of the Byzantine Empire. Now West European states began pinning their hopes on Moscow in their struggle against Turkish domination. It was at that time that the legend emerged according to which Moscow, just like Rome, lay on seven hills.

Grand Prince Ivan III, Dmitri Donskoi's great-grandson, accepted the proposal made to him by the Papal diplomats and married Sophia (Zoë) Palaeologus, a relative and, in a sense, successor of the Byzantine emperors, for this matrimonial alliance enhanced the international prestige of the Moscow state, but he did not in any way comply with their wishes in his foreign policy. The Tatars, Lithuania and the Livonian Order remained his principal enemies. In 1480, the Tatar yoke was finally thrown off. The process of political unification of the Russian lands was making rapid progress. Relations were established with the Venetian republic, Turkey, Hungary, Denmark, and Persia. Ivan III and his associates had a clear idea of what the capital of the young state should look like so that it could represent Muscovy in a befitting way. The Kremlin obviously needed a new, improved system of fortifications. The plans for its reconstruction developed at the time incorporated every technical innovation of the day, from the new building material, bricks, to the latest inventions of West European engineers. And, since specialists from Northern Italy were reputed to be the best, it was they who were invited to Moscow in the 1480s.

It was decided once more to build the new Kremlin without demolishing the old walls. The new walls went up much further out and thus the area covered by the fortress was once more increased. As estimated by archeologists, the 12th-century citadel had covered an area of some 3 hectares; now its walls enclosed an area of 28 hectares and were 2,235 metres long. The first fortification of its kind in the practice of Moscow master builders, the Kremlin with its technical features and architectural treatment became a model for Russian builders, wherever they had to work, for many decades to come. This influence was all the more significant as, after the unification of the Russian lands into a single Moscow state in the 16th century, it was now Moscow itself and not local liege princes that had to take care of the construction of fortifications throughout the territory.

At the time when the reconstruction of the Kremlin, supervised by the Italian engineer Alevisio Stary (Old), was being completed, a highly sophisticated system of water-development works was built, making it possible to divert the waters of the Neglinnaya River from the Kremlin and, at the same time, to create a reliable water obstacle in the case of an enemy attack. It included a deep moat, a chain of sluiced ponds and dams to maintain the water level on the side of what is now the Manège, a number of bridges in front of the Kremlin's gates (only one of them, the bridge in front of the Troitsky Gate terminating in a bridgehead, the Kutafya Tower, has survived to this day). By 1516, the work was completed and a new bed for the Neglinnaya River was dug from the Borovitsky Gate along the Kremlin wall, for the natural riverbed made a sharp turn to the southwest and the Neglinnaya joined the Moskva River at a spot near today's Moskva Open-Air Swimming Pool at the Kropotkin Gate.

But the Kremlin walls did not long remain the only stone protection of Moscow. In 1538, the stone walls of the Kitaigorod adjoining the Kremlin were built under the supervision of master builder Petrok Maly. In 1586-1593, shortly before the Polish-Swedish intervention, Fyodor Kon and his associates, who had won fame for building the kremlin (citadel) in Smolensk, built the walls of the Bely Gorod, the White City (today the Boulevard Ring of Moscow), with a total length of 10 kilometres and with 27 towers, ten of which were provided with gateways.

In writing about the position and role of the Moscow Kremlin, the Englishman Giles Fletcher, who stayed in Moscow for some time at the end of the 16th century and might be called an authority on the subject, noted that its inner wall and the structures it enclosed (which were as safe here as the heart is inside the body), washed by the Moskva River flowing next to the wall, were called the Czar's castle. He also observed that at the time Moscow was somewhat larger than London.

The Kremlin was built and rebuilt and the city **posad** round it was growing rapidly. In the early 15th century it was limited to the area of the Kitaigorod and by the end of that century it already included numerous **slobodi** (artisans' quarters) as well. From the mid-15th century, the Moscow chronicles noted the emergence of stone churches and public buildings in the **slobodi**. A number of stone churches were built in the **posad**. One of them, the Church of the Conception of St. Anne "at the Corner", is still to be seen today on the bank of the Moskva River at the southeast side of the Rossiya Hotel. Alevisio Novy (New), the builder of the Archangel Cathedral in the Moscow Kremlin, built ten churches in the **posad** in addition to those which he built for the Grand Prince.

Cities in the land of Muscovy were different yet they had certain features in common. The city centres often resembled each other and many were based on the layout that had been developed in the Moscow Kremlin. Some of the features which dated to the 14th and 15th centuries were subsequently used in 18th-century and, even 19th-century town planning.

The main cathedral — the Cathedral of the Dormition in the case of the Moscow Kremlin — had a massive and clear-cut silhouette. Next to it on the southeast side was the vertical of a bell tower, or a church performing the same function, and on the southwest side was the Prince's palace. The part facing the cathedral was intended for ceremonies and official solemnities and inevitably had a Red Porch (grand entrance). Accordingly, the south door of the cathedral was the Prince's door and the one on the west, the Metropolitan's door, since the chambers of the hierarch were located nearby.

The square in front of the cathedral was the town's main square and thus it became the centre of public life. From the cathedral square, streets fanned out radially towards the town gates just as they did in the Kremlin, changing into major thoroughfares beyond its walls. In Moscow, the traditional names of a number of streets such as Tverskaya Street (now Gorky Street), Bolshaya Dmitrovka Street (now Pushkinskaya Street), Kaluzhskaya Street (now Leninsky Prospekt), Bolshaya Serpukhovskaya Street, and others remind one of this fact.

In the 17th century, the Moscow state maintained far-flung diplomatic relations and numerous foreigners lived on its lands, in particular, in the city of Moscow. By the mid-17th century, the population of Moscow reached 200,000, including 28,000 foreigners. Among them were specialists of every kind ranging from medical doctors to fortifiers, from engineers to musicians, and from merchants to wig-makers. The right to enter Moscow was granted only to representatives of the trades needed by the state.

Peter the Great's rise to power at the end of the 17th century initially meant an acceleration in construction work in Moscow. The great fire of 1701, which destroyed most buildings in the Kremlin, also played a part. Peter the Great gave orders that most of the new buildings erected on the vacant plots were to be secular. The most remarkable example is the Arsenal, an imposing structure towering above the Kremlin walls. Originally intended as a place for storing weapons, it subsequently became the first museum of Russian military trophies. However, after the foundation of St. Petersburg in 1703 and the transferral of the capital there in 1712, construction work in Moscow was not only reduced but outright suspended. The

city on the Neva River was in dire need of builders and building materials for the czar's new projects and as a result, between 1714 and 1728 all construction of stone buildings was prohibited in Moscow. Yet even after the ban was lifted, it took some time for things to return to normal. Although Moscow did not actually become a provincial town, it did take advantage of this opportunity to preserve and develop its 17th-century characteristics. While the city continued to be a major trading centre and the growth of industry continued to accelerate, it also became a kind of place of exile for those members of the nobility who were malcontent or who fell into disfavour with the court. Living here so far from the czar and his court, they made every effort to demonstrate their independence by their way of life. That is why Moscow at the time consisted mostly of urban estates where the manor house was surrounded by various service buildings, often with a large garden-park containing various attractions such as pavilions, artificial grottoes, summerhouses, sculpture, ponds, fountains, and open-air theatres, which adjoined the front yard or, as it was called in the French manner, the **cour d'honneur.**

Still another feature of that Moscow of landowners was the fact that both the manor house and the gardens on every estate could be freely used by the Muscovites. Even noblemen who barely knew the lord of the manor might pay him a call, and as for his gardens, Muscovites from all walks of life had the use of the facilities. There were hundreds of such garden-parks in the city and the owners considered it a matter of honour to keep their fellow Muscovites interested in them. Best conforming to these conditions of life in Moscow was the creative work of Matvei Kazakov, one of the best-known and most talented local architects.

The stay of Napoleon's Grande Armée in Moscow for a month and a half in 1812 inflicted innumerable losses upon the city. The fires of 1812, which destroyed or damaged most buildings in the centre of the city, brought about the ruin of quite a few of their former owners. Industrialists and merchants replaced the noble proprietors of the Moscow manors. The biggest and most luxurious estates were bought by the city for its needs. In most cases they were converted into city hospitals, and the State Assignation Bank was housed in the former manor house of the Lunins in Suvorovsky Boulevard.

Characteristic of new private mansions built after the fires of 1812 was their rather modest appearance. The tendency is particularly evident in the works of the leading Moscow architects of the first quarter of the 19th century such as Domenico Gilardi, Afanasi Grigoryev, and others. Yet even in those parts of the city where the so-called row houses predominated (i.e. houses built along the frontal lines of the streets and often joined by a common wall), an echo of the amenities of former estates could be found in the green inner courtyards, which looked more like gardens. The urban estate was now enclosed, as it were, within the mansion that faced on the adjoining plot of land which could not be seen from the street. Particularly characteristic in this respect was the merchant district of Moscow, separated from the city centre by the Moskva River, known as the Zamoskvorechye, so colourfully described by the celebrated Russian playwright Alexander Ostrovsky. An example of everyday life in the Zamoskvorechye in the middle and second half of the 19th century is to be seen in the playwright's memorial house-museum in Ostrovsky Street.

The abolition of serfdom in the early 1860s gave a fresh powerful impetus to the urban development of Moscow and stepped up the rate of construction work in the city. Alongside the mansions of financial tycoons, who often employed the

architect Fyodor Shekhtel, innumerable tenement houses of an original architecture were built, in many ways reminiscent of the contemporary trends in tenement construction in West European countries. The most striking trend in Moscow architecture of the period was Russian Art Nouveau, whose brilliant examples include the Metropol and National hotels, the buildings in Kuznetsky Most Street, Petrovka Street, Petrovskiye Linii (Lane), and Pushkinskaya Street.

After the October Revolution of 1917, constructivism represented by such talented architects as Melnikov came to the fore. Of no less interest is the legacy of the architect Ivan Leonidov, who is well-known to builders, even though he had little chance to put his creative ideas into practice. The relatively small number of constructivist structures to be seen in Moscow is explained by the complexity of the historical period during which they were built. This was conditioned by a shortage both of quality building materials and of skilled builders. It cost the country great effort to adapt itself first to the New Economic Policy (NEP) and then to the departure from it.

The architecture of Moscow, like an immense book, enables one to read the history of the country and the people, page after page. This publication proposes to help the reader in his task by providing pages from the history of the city's architecture and at the same time, by portraying the people who wrote these pages with their lives and their talent.

Nina Moleva

RED SQUARE

Stretching along one side of the Kremlin walls, Red Square has become an integral part of this architectural ensemble.

Until late in the 15th century, the buildings of the **posad** (trading quarter) came almost right up to the wall. When the great fire of 1493 laid bare a vast area between the Kremlin and the city Torg (Mart), it was left vacant and was turned into a market centre. At first, the site of the future square was called the Pozhar (Burnt-Out Place). It lay between the two main districts of the city centre, the Kremlin and the Kitaigorod, and was bounded on the west by the Kremlin moat and on the east by the Torg, (the site of the Pozhar had long been regarded as part of the Torg). On the south, the square was delimited by a steep slope on the top of which stood a Trinity Church with a small graveyard. After the Cathedral of the Intercession-on-the-Moat was built in the mid-16th century, in the reign of Ivan the Terrible, the part of the square adjacent to it became firmly established in its role as the hub of Moscow.

Near the cathedral on the **vzlobye** (crest) of the hill a platform known as the Lobnoye Mesto (meaning a "place that can be seen from all around") was built in 1534. From this platform, the czar and top clergymen spoke to the people on grand occasions. Tradition has it that young Ivan the Terrible addressed the people from this platform in 1547 after a devastating fire in Moscow. It was also here that Prince Vasili Shuisky swore before the people in 1604 that czarevich Dmitri, son of Ivan the Terrible, had been killed. On May 17, 1606, the body of False Dmitri I was displayed near the Lobnoye Mesto and it was from here that Prince Dmitri Pozharsky proclaimed in 1612 the freedom of Moscow from foreign invasion. In 1786, the Lobnoye Mesto was rebuilt by the architect Matvei Kazakov.

In the second half of the 17th century, after the Cathedral of St. Basil the Blessed and a number of stone shops (later on replaced by the Upper Shopping Arcade, which is now the GUM State Department Store) had been built and the tall hipped roofs were added to the Spasskaya Tower and the other Kremlin towers, the trading square acquired a solemn, grand appearance. It was then that the people began to call it Krasnaya, which in those days meant beautiful and now means red.

The History Museum

Top: Ressurection Gate with the Chapel of the Iberian Icon of Our Lady, built from a scratch in 1994-95; part of a chapel. Bottom: Church of Our Lady of Kazan, built from a scratch in 1993

◀ *Views of Red Square*

THE CATHEDRAL OF THE INTERCESSION (CATHEDRAL OF ST. BASIL THE BLESSED)

On the south side of Red Square the particoloured cupolas of the Cathedral of the Intercession, better known as the Cathedral of St. Basil the Blessed, a wonderful creation of Old Russian architecture, rise high picturesquely. It was built as a monument to a major turning point in Russian history, the defeat of the Kazan Khanate (1552-1554). After each major victory, a small wooden church was erected near the Trinity Church which already stood here, in honour of the saint on whose feast day the victory was won. Thus, by the end of the war, there were eight churches on this site. After the final victory, Ivan the Terrible, on the advice of Metropolitan Makary, ordered stone churches to be built in place of the wooden ones. Barma and Posnik, the master builders commissioned by the czar to do the job (there are reasons to assume that they were, in fact, one person), however, created a monument whose composition has no parallel in the entire history of world architecture. They built eight pillarlike churches on a single foundation, placed symmetrically round the ninth, central pillar crowned with a tentlike roof, which is the tallest and architecturally the most complex. The central church was dedicated to the Feast of the Intercession of Our Lady, celebrated on October 1, the day when the walls of Kazan were blown up and the city was taken by assault. That is why the entire cathedral was named the Cathedral of the Intercession. Construction which employed bricks, a relatively new building material at the time, lasted from 1555 to 1561. The foundation, the base and some of the decorative elements were made of white stone. The cathedral is striking in the diversity of its architectural forms and the flights of imagination displayed by its creators: each of the cathedral's pillars differs from the others. Until the additions made to the Bell Tower of Ivan the Great, it was the tallest structure in Moscow and from the moment of its appearance it became the most popular church in town.

From the very beginning the cathedral had no clearly defined main façade. The building was intended to be seen from all sides and to be walked around both on the outside and on the inside. In contrast to the monumental outward appearance, the interiors create an impression of a narrow labyrinth interrupted by the vertical inner spaces of the pillar churches. The biggest of them, the pillar of the Church of the Intercession (height, 46 metres above floor level), has an inside floor area of 64 square metres.

The cathedral retained its original shape until 1588, when a tenth church was added over the grave of Vasili (Basil) the Blessed, a Jester of the Lord well-known in Moscow at the time, on the northwest side. Ever since, the Cathedral of the Intercession has been known as the Cathedral of St. Basil the Blessed.

During restoration work in 1954-1955, when part of the brick facing of the walls eroded by the wind was replaced, a system which had made it possible to erect such a complex building without graphic drawings, formerly unknown in Russian architecture, was uncovered. All the walls of the building are pierced with wooden constructions which acted as a sort of "spatial drawing". The rather slender beams joined together both horizontally and vertically were used to outline the silhouette of the future building before bricklaying was started and to indicate the size and position of all its architectural and decorative elements.

The cathedral has become an integral part of the ensemble of Red Square and one of its most vivid adornments.

THE MONUMENT TO MININ AND POZHARSKY

Next to the Cathedral of St. Basil the Blessed stands the monument to Kozma Minin and Dmitri Pozharsky, the heroes of the national struggle for liberation against the Swedish and Polish invaders in 1610-1612. This was the first sculptural monument erected in Moscow. It was put up in 1818 with money raised by public subscription. True to the classical traditions of the time, the famous sculptor, Ivan Martos, clothed his heroes in Grecian garb. High-relief scenes on the bronze plaques set into the pedestal show the people of Nizhny Novgorod donating money and valuables for the army, and the Russians driving out the Poles. The inscription on the pedestal reads: "To Citizen Minin and Prince Pozharsky from a grateful Russia 1818".

The Cathedral of St. Basil the Blessed. 1555-61, ▶
architects Barma and Posnik

View of the Cathedral of St. Basil
the Blessed from the Kremlin

The monument to Kozma Minin and Dmitri Pozharsky.
1818, sculptor Ivan Martos

A panoramic view of Moscow and the Kremlin

THE KREMLIN

The Moscow Kremlin is the chief architectural ensemble of the city. It has few rivals in the number of unique masterpieces or architecture and other arts concentrated within its walls. The skyline of the Kremlin is strikingly majestic and picturesque. The might of its walls, its ridge-roofed towers and the three-dimensional expressiveness of the buildings clustered on its grounds offer panoramas of rare beauty.

The irregular triangle of the Kremlin walls, repeating the outline of Borovitsky Cape, encloses an area of 27.5 hectares. The maximum height of the hill above the level of the Moskva River is about 25 metres.

The ensemble of the Moscow Kremlin is the result of the efforts of many generations. Initially, it was a small fortified settlement which sprang up on Borovitsky Hill — a promontory at the spot where the Neglinnaya River flowed into

the Moskva River. The oldest archaeological finds unearthed on the Kremlin grounds date back to the Bronze Age. Signs of a Slavic settlement here date to no later than the end of the 11th century. At the time, the fortress on the top of Borovitsky Hill covered an area of about 5 hectares.

The first Moscow fortifications consisted of a moat, a rampart and a palisade. At first, the fortress was called simply **grad** (city) or **grad Moskva** (the city of Moscow).

The city built here on the orders of Prince Yuri Dolgoruky in the 12th century was 5 to 6 times as large as the initial area. In the 14th century, during the rule of Ivan Kalita, when Moscow became the centre of a Grand Principality, the fortress — the seat of the Grand Prince of Moscow — was for the first time perceived as a separate, principal part of the city, as its nucleus. The chronicles indicate that the fortress was given a name of

its own, the Kremlin (Citadel), in 1331. In 1339-1340, new walls and towers of oak were erected and in 1366-1368, during the rule of Dmitri Donskoi, a mighty white-stone citadel was built here.

The intensive construction work in the Kremlin as a result of which Moscow came to be known as the "white-stone city" was carried on against the background of struggles with the Golden Horde and Lithuania and rivalry with Tver. Before long the new Kremlin successfully repulsed attacks of the armies of Grand Prince Olgerd of Lithuania (in 1368 and 1370). True, in 1380-1382 Khan Tokhtamysh attacked Moscow and with a ruse broke into the Kremlin, but the citadel, and the rest of the city, was soon rebuilt. By the end of the 14th century, the Kremlin was tightly packed with various structures. The whole of its grounds was covered

with churches, monasteries and manors of the Grand Prince's retainers, top military men and rich merchants.

The 15th century was marked by further growth of Moscow's political and military might. By the end of the 15th century, the unification of the Russian feudal principalities under the authority of Moscow was, in the main, completed. A single Russian state had been formed. Grand Prince Ivan III of Moscow became the Grand Prince of All Russia.

Ivan III launched reconstruction of the Kremlin on a grand scale, having invited a number of noted master builders from Italy for the purpose. At the time, Italian builders were recognised as the best in Europe. And, so, alongside builders from Pskov, Novgorod and Vladimir who had come to the capital on the orders of the Grand

Cathedral Square. View of the Cathedral of the Dormition, the Patriarch's Palace and the Cathedral of the Twelve Apostles

Prince to take part in the construction of the city, the Italian architect and military engineer Aristotile Fioravanti arrived in Moscow together with his son Andrea and his apprentice Pietro.

The new Cathedral of the Dormition (1475-1479) was the first to be built. In 1484-1489, the festive Cathedral of the Annunciation was erected next to it. Subsequently, in 1505-1508, they were joined by the Cathedral of the Archangel.

This is how this remarkable ensemble of Cathedral Square, the oldest square in Moscow, with its three cathedrals and the snow-white Bell Tower of Ivan the Great took shape. Still another adornment of the square is the Palace of Facets, the formal reception room of the Grand Prince's palace, built by Marco Ruffo (Fryazin) and Pietro Antonio Solari (Pyotr Fryazin) in 1487-1491. At the turn of the 16th century, the Kremlin was practically completely renovated: at the time, new Kremlin walls were built in parallel with the construction of the palace and the cathedrals. For a whole decade, starting from 1485, the dilapidated white-stone walls and towers were gradually pulled down and replaced with new ones. The construction work was supervised by Italian architects. It was then that the Kremlin acquired its present-day outlines.

The fortress walls, forming an irregular triangle, are 2,235 m long, from 3.5 to 6.5 m thick and from 5 to 19 m high. Atop the walls stand 1,045 bifurcated merlons, from 2 to 2.5 metres in height and fitted with narrow embrasures. Behind the merlons and running inside the wall is a combat platform from 2 to 4 metres wide.

Along the east Kremlin wall facing what is now the Red Square a moat, 12 m deep and 32 m wide, was dug and filled with water. On its northwest side Borovitsky Hill was protected by the Neglinnaya River and on its south side, by the Moskva River. Thus the Kremlin fortress was surrounded by water on all sides like an island and could be entered only by way of drawbridges. The Kremlin was a superb example of the fortification art of the period.

THE KREMLIN WALLS AND TOWERS

The first thing which arrests our attention when we look at the Kremlin and which immediately arouses our admiration is its walls and towers. Their construction was supervised by the Italian master builders Anton Fryazin, Marco Ruffo (Fryazin), Antonio Gilardi, Pietro Antonio Solari, and Aloisio (Alevisio) di Carcano, specially invited for the purpose.

There are 18 towers in the Kremlin wall. The Tainitskaya Tower (Tower of Secrets), the oldest one in the Kremlin, was built in 1485. As indicated by the name, the tower contained a secret well and a secret underground passage to the river bank. And the last to be built, the Tsarskaya (Czar's) Tower — a small tentlike turret built right on top of the wall between the Spasskaya (Saviour's) and Nabatnaya (Tocsin) Tower — acquired its present-day appearance in 1680. From here, according to tradition, the czar would watch important events taking place in Red Square.

The tallest tower in the Kremlin is the Troitskaya (Trinity) Tower which is 80 metres high, including the star. In front of its stands the Kutafya Tower, the lowest in the Kremlin (height 13.5 m), looking as if it were made of white lace. It is the only bridgehead watchtower to have survived to this day.

The three corner towers are round in shape. The first one, the Vodovzvodnaya (Water) Tower, stands near the Bolshoi Kamenny Bridge. It was named thus because it was the first tower in Moscow in which a machine for drawing up water was installed, supplying the Kremlin palaces and upper gardens with water from the Moskva River. This tower, built at the end of 1488, is almost 59 metres high.

It was also then that the second corner tower, the Beklemishev Tower (height, 46.2 m), was built. Sometimes called the Moskvoretskaya Tower because of its proximity to the Moskvoretsky Bridge, it traditionally seems to have been

View of the Kremlin from the Moskva River

named after Boyar Beklemishev, whose manor was located in the vicinity.

The third corner tower, the Uglovaya Arsenalnaya (Corner Arsenal) or Sobakin Tower, stands next to Kremlin Passage. It took its name from the Arsenal, right behind it. This 60 m high tower has deep foundations and its walls are as much as 5 metres thick. The secret spring it contains is still in existence today.

The most remarkable of all the Kremlin towers is the Spasskaya (Saviour's) Tower, known as the Frolovskaya (St. Frol's) Tower until the 17th century, built in 1491 under the supervision of Pietro Antonio Solari. The gate has for centuries been the main official entrance to the Kremlin.

In the 16th and 17th centuries, the Spassky Gate was used for ceremonial processions made by the Czar and the Patriarch and for meeting foreign ambassadors. The street leading from the gate to Cathedral Square was the main street of the Kremlin. In 1624-1625, the octagonal multitiered turret which now surmounts the rectangular tower was built by the Russian master builder Bazhen Ogurtsov and the English clockmaker Christopher Halloway. It was also then that the first clock made to the design of Christopher Halloway was installed in the turret.

Today the tower is 67.3 metres high and its three upper tiers house the mechanism of the clock. The one now to be seen under the pointed roof of the Spasskaya Tower is the fourth in line and was built by the brothers Butenop, who used various parts of the older clock, and installed it in 1851-1852. The mechanism itself weighs about 25 tons. The clock chimes every quarter of an hour with the melodious sound of its nine quarter bells and booms on the hour with its big hour bell weighing 2,160 kg. The length of the minute hand, the biggest one, is 3.28 metres. The clock is wound twice a day and shows Moscow Time used as the basis for standard time throughout the country.

A true masterpiece of Old Russian architecture, this tower, one of the most beautiful in the Kremlin, strikes the eye with the exquisite elegance of its carved white-stone ornamentation.

The Nikolskaya (St. Nicholas') Tower (67.1 m), standing near the History Museum and decorated with a lacework of white-stone carving, was built at the same time as the Spasskaya Tower.

The next gate tower, the Troitskaya (Trinity) Tower, rises above the Alexandrovsky Gardens. It is connected with the openwork Kutafya Tower by a stone bridge which once spanned the Neglinnaya River before its course was diverted into a pipe laid down under the Alexandrovsky Gardens. The

Part of the Kremlin wall

The Nikolskaya (St. Nicholas') Tower

Troitskaya Tower was built in 1495-1499.

Next to the Armoury is the Borovitskaya Tower (50.7 m), built in 1490. Nearby, the remains of the earthwork built on the orders of Peter the Great during the war with Sweden are still to be seen.

Almost all the Kremlin towers have a glorious history. The Konstantino-Yeleninskaya Tower (Tower of Sts. Constantine and Helen), which is between the Spasskaya and Moskvoretskaya Towers, stands on the site of the white-stone Timofeyev Tower through whose gate Dmitri Donskoi led his troops in 1380 to the historic Battle of Kulikovo.

In 1612, the people's volunteer army led by Kozma Minin and Dmitri Pozharsky fought their way into the Kremlin through the Nikolsky and Spassky Gates and ousted the Polish interventionists. In 1812, the upper part of the Nikolskaya Tower was blown up by the retreating French, but four years later it was completely restored. The Nabatnaya (Tocsin) Tower, standing opposite the Cathedral of St. Basil the Blessed, took its name from the tocsin which used to hang under its tentlike roof. Any sign of enemy detachments approaching the capital via the Serpukhov or Kaluga Roads, set off the alarm and the bell resounded over the whole city. In 1771, during the revolt in Moscow known as the Plague Rebellion, the insurgents summoned the townsfolk to the Kremlin by sounding the tocsin. After the revolt had been put down, Empress Catherine the Great ordered the clapper to be removed. In 1803, the bell was taken down and is now kept in the Armoury.

In 1935, four of the Kremlin towers — the Spasskaya, Nikolskaya, Troitskaya, and Borovitskaya — were topped with five-pointed stars of stainless steel and copper. In 1937, they were replaced with glowing red stars and a fifth star was mounted on the Vodovzvodnaya Tower.

When seen from below, from the ground, the stars do not seem particularly large, yet the points of each one are 3 to 3.75 metres apart. The lighting inside the stars is controlled from a room in the Troitskaya Tower. The framework of the stars is made of stainless steel and they are faced in special three-layer glass which is ruby-red on the outside and milk-white on the inside. Each star is lit by a 3,700 to 5,000 watt bulb and, to protect the bulbs from overheating, cooled air is forced into the stars through hollow rods 24 hours a day. The stars are so designed that they can revolve smoothly in the wind.

The St. George Icon from the Cathedral of the Dormition. Late 11th-early 12th centuries

from the 11th to the 17th century is of enormous historical and artistic value. Soviet restorers have uncovered part of the original 15th-16th century murals, which had once been thought irrevocably lost.

The cathedral also contains many remarkable works of applied art. Standing near the south entrance is the czar's seat of Ivan the Terrible made of carved wood in the form of a square bower topped with a multitiered tentlike roof and supported by four lions also carved of wood. This masterpiece of Russian wood-carving, known as the Throne of the Monomachus, was made in 1551. The panels of its enclosure are decorated with carved reliefs illustrating the story of Prince Vladimir Monomachus' Thracian campaign. The white-stone patriarchal seat adorned with picturesque ornamentation also dates from the 16th century. Standing in the southwest corner of the cathedral is a canopy of cast bronze openwork encasing a shrine with holy relics, made in 1624 by master foundryman Dmitri Sverchkov.

The cathedral is illuminated by 12 chandeliers made of gilt bronze and a number of multitiered candelabra (17th century).

The Cathedral of the Dormition. 1475-79 ▶

A bronze canopy. 1624

THE CATHEDRAL OF THE DORMITION

The Cathedral of the Dormition stands on the site of Moscow's first stone cathedral built by Ivan Kalita in the 14th century, which in turn replaced churches that were even older — a wooden structure dating to the 12th-century and a 13-th century building in stone. The largest edifice of its time in Russia, the Cathedral of the Dormition was built in 1475-1479 under the supervision of the Italian architect Aristotile Fioravanti after the model of the 12th-century Cathedral of the Dormition in the ancient Russian city of Vladimir. The perfect proportions and five gilt domes endowed it with an integrity and grandeur that was monolithic in appearance. In the 16th and 17th centuries, the cathedral was widely used as a model by the Russian architects.

For four centuries the Cathedral of the Dormition remained the main cathedral in Russia. It was here that czars and emperors were crowned, important ceremonies held and Moscow metropolitans and patriarchs consecrated and, upon their demise, buried (their tombs lie along the walls).

The central part of the cathedral is separated from the chancel by a five-tiered iconostasis (17th century) which is approximately 16 metres high and which was covered in the late 19th century with embossed gilt silver. This collection of icons

The Nativity of Christ altar Icon from the Cathedral of the Annunciation. By Andrei Rublyov

faced in ornamental agate-coloured jasper brought here on the orders of Ivan the Terrible from a cathedral in the city of Rostov.

The first frescoes in the cathedral were executed in 1508 by a group of artists headed by Theodosius, son of the gifted painter Dionysius. The frescoes were badly damaged by time and fire and were frequently repainted and disfigured over the centuries. For a long time they were considered to have been irretrievably lost, but Soviet restorers have succeeded in uncovering part of the 16th-century masterpieces. Those which have survived best include the composition **The Liberation of Peter from Prison,** as well as **St. Demetrius of Salonica,** which are to be seen on the southwest column of the cathedral. There is also an interesting fresco on the south wall of the north gallery showing a number of scenes from the life of the prophet Jonah and his stay in the great fish's belly.

The murals on the vaults of the north gallery furnish an idea of the cultural interests of our ancestors in the 15th and 16th centuries and the broadness of their outlook. Here you can see conventional portraits of ancient philosophers, scholars and historians such as Aristotle, Anacharsis, Menander, Ptolemy, Thucydides, and Plutarch. And shown on the pilasters between the walls are representations of Virgil, Homer, and others.

The cathedral's multitiered iconostasis is of unique historical and artistic value. It was executed in 1405 for the older stone Church of the Annunciation. The general concept of the iconostasis and many of its icons are by Theophanes the Greek, one of the greatest painters of the period. They include images of Jesus Christ, the Mother of God, St. John the Baptist, St. Gabriel the Archangel, St. Paul the Apostle, St. Basil the Great, and St. John Chrysostom, placed on the second tier. On the third tier, works by Andrei Rublyov, one of the world's greatest artists, are to be seen. Rublyov's works are distinguished by lyricism, profound humanitarianism, noble spirituality, and unique harmony of colours and the artistic form. The icons painted by Rublyov are in the left part of the tier. They include **The Annunciation, The Nativity of Our Lord Jesus Christ, The Purification of Our Lady. The Epiphany, The Transfiguration, The Raising of Lazarus from the Dead,** and **The Entry into Jerusalem.** The third artist of the icons which are to be seen here is Prokhor of Gorodets.

THE CATHEDRAL OF THE ANNUNCIATION

The Cathedral of the Annunciation unites in one artistic whole the works of 14th-16th century Russian masters. The white-stone foundation and crypt of the cathedral are the surviving parts of the older Church of the Annunciation built in the late 14th and early 15th centuries. In 1484-1489, in the reign of Ivan III, masons from Pskov built a new triple-domed brick church on the old foundation. In 1562-1564, four side chapels with domes were built upon the cathedral's galleries and two false domes were added above the oldest eastern part. Thus the cathedral became a nine-domed edifice. Both the domes and the entire roof were gilded, and so the cathedral became popularly known as "the gold-headed".

The Cathedral of the Annunciation, which was in the days of old connected with the royal chambers by a passage and served as the private chapel of the royal family, is not very large. It has beautiful portals leading from the parvis to the central part of the cathedral. The south portal, the oldest of the three, is framed with columns. The north and west portals (16th century), lavishly decorated with carved and gilded ornamentation on a bright-blue background, have a more festive appearance. The window frames and the columns of the gallery are also decorated with carving. The floor of the cathedral is

The Cathedral of the Annunciation. ▶
14th-15th centuries

THE CATHEDRAL
OF ST. MICHAEL THE ARCHANGEL

The five-domed Cathedral of St. Michael the Archangel, the second largest cathedral in the Kremlin, was built in 1505-1508 on the site of an ancient cathedral of the same name by the architect Alevisio Fryazin Novy, invited from Italy, in the style of traditional Russian architecture. The rich decoration in the cathedral and the splendour of its architectural shapes, however, are more characteristic of the Italian Renaissance.

The original murals have not been preserved, for they deteriorated and had been removed together with the plaster by the middle of the 17th century. The new frescoes were painted in 1652-1666 from tracings of the original murals made by a group of artists called in from various Russian towns and by master painters of the Moscow Armoury, Simon Ushakov, Stepan of Ryazan and Fyodor Zubov. They displayed great skill in depicting battle scenes from the history of the Russian people's struggle for national independence, as well as scenes from everyday life and Biblical subjects.

For more than 300 years the Cathedral of St. Michael the Archangel was the burial place of the Moscow grand princes and czars. The white-stone tomb slabs bear epitaphs engraved in intricate Slavonic characters with the names and dates of the deceased. To ensure their better preservation, bronze encasements with glass panes in them were placed over the tombs in the early 20th century. The oldest tomb is that of Ivan Kalita, who died in 1340. In the neighbouring tombs Dmitri Donskoi, Ivan II, and Ivan IV the Terrible and his sons lie buried.

The murals include full-length portraits of the Moscow grand princes. On the southwest column is a picture of Alexander Nevsky, the great Russian military leader who became famous through the rout of the Swedes on the Neva River in 1240 and of the German knights on the ice of Lake Chudskoye in 1242. The cathedral's iconostasis, put up in 1813, contains icons dating from the 16th and 17th centuries. On its first tier are monuments of Old Russian icon-painting, which include the icon of **St. Michael the Archangel.** The heavenly patron of Russian warriors is shown in full armour and with a drawn sword and his stern countenance breathes confidence in victory over the enemy.

The Cathedral of St. Michael the Archangel caught the imagination of Old Russian master builders. Under the influence of its architecture, an original style which further developed the motifs of its décor emerged in Russia in the second half of the 16th century.

The Grand Prince Alexander Nevsky fresco on the southwest pillar

Stone tombs of the great Russian princes and czars

◀ *The Cathedral of St. Michael the Archangel. 1505-08*

*View of the Cathedral of the Annunciation
and the Palace of Facets. In the background:
the Grand Kremlin Palace*

*Part of the façade
of the Palace of Facets*

◀ *The Bell Tower of Ivan
the Great. 16th century*

THE PALACE OF FACETS

The Palace of Facets, the ceremonial throne room of the palace
of the czars built at the end of the 15th century, is one of the
few remaining parts and one of the oldest stone civic buildings
in Moscow. It was built in 1487-1491 by Russian craftsmen
working under the Italian architects Marco Ruffo Fryazin and
Pietro Antonio Solari. The main façade of the building overlooking Cathedral Square is faced in cut stone slabs, from
which the name derives. The spacious square hall is 9 metres
high at the uppermost point of the vault and has an area of 495
square metres, which made it the largest hall in Moscow at the
time of its completion. The cruciform vaults of the Palace of
Facets are supported by a rectangular pillar in the centre of the

hall. On the walls and on the vaults are reproductions of ancient murals executed in 1881 by the Belousov brothers, masters from Palekh (a village renowned for its distinctive paintings). At the Palace of Facets, formal ceremonies were held, foreign ambassadors were received and the sittings of the Zemsky Sobor (National Assembly) took place. It was in 1653, at one of such sittings, that the Zemsky Sobor adopted the decision on the unification of the Ukraine with Russia. It was here, too, that Ivan the Terrible celebrated the capture of Kazan in 1552 and Peter the Great marked Russia's victory over the Swedes at Poltava in 1709.

Following a number of fires and repairs, the appearance of the Palace of Facets changed to a certain extent. In 1696, a fire destroyed its high gilt hipped roof decorated with a coloured pattern. The windows with their splendid frames decorated with carved columns, made by the noted architect Osip Startsev, date from a later period. For some time after the Grand Kremlin Palace was built, the entrance to the Palace of Facets was from Cathedral Square and the Red (grand) Porch with stone lions was subsequently pulled down. Today the only way to the Sacred Vestibule of the Palace of Facets is through the Vladimirsky (St. Vladimir's) Hall of the Grand Kremlin Palace. The Sacred Vestibule is decorated with white-stone portals which look as if they were entwined with gold and silver latticework — such was the craft of the Russian stonecarvers. On the second floor above the vestibule, the window of a **tainik** (secret chamber) can be seen. It was here that the czarinas and princesses would watch the ceremonies taking place in the Palace of Facets, since

custom prevented women from participating in them. This custom was broken only by Peter the Great, who ordered women to be present at all celebrations and feasts.

In our day, skilful masters have restored the stone carving and paintings on the walls and on the vaults and renovated the three-tiered crystal chandeliers and the window surrounds done in relief. The central pillar of the hall has also been restored. In the 15th century, it was faced with white-stone slabs decorated with gilded carving. In the 18th century, the damaged, carving was removed and the sides of the column were decorated with ornamental painting to simulate stone carving. Restorers succeeded in finding fragments of the original alabaster reliefs in the storerooms of the former Rumyantsev Museum, and carvers then copied the ancient carving.

Interiors of the Palace of Facets. Walls and vaults painted by the Belousov brothers, masters from the village of Palekh

Wall painting depicting Russian Grand Princes. Detail

The Grand Kremlin Palace. Mid-19th century

THE GRAND KREMLIN PALACE

The Grand Kremlin Palace stands on the crest of Borovitsky Hill in the southern part of the Kremlin, where the grand prince's palatial estate used to be in the days of old. In the reign of Ivan Kalita it consisted of numerous log houses with porches and turrets interconnected by vestibules, stairways and passages. Ivan III built the first stone palace here. The buildings on the Kremlin grounds were more than once destroyed as a result of fire and enemy raids and replaced with new ones. Under Ivan the Terrible fire broke out twice in the palace and each time new structures were added in the process of restoration. The striking skyline of the Kremlin, the abundance of gilt and the bright colours made it look like a town out of a fairy tale. But soon the significance of the Kremlin changed dramatically. Peter the Great built a new palace in Lefortovo. And when the new capital began to rise on the Neva River, all construction work in Moscow, the Kremlin included, was temporarily discontinued. It was not until the 1740s that the famous architect Bartolomeo Rastrelli, commissioned by Empress Elizabeth Petrovna, renovated the czar's palace which had fallen into decay and erected a splendidly ornamental building on the old 15th-century foundations.

The construction of the present Grand Kremlin Palace was started in 1839 and lasted 11 years. Czar Nicholas I, in whose reign it was built, intended to emphasize the idea of greatness of the Russian autocracy by the immense size of the building. The new palace was 125 metres long and had a total floor area of some 25,000 square metres. It contains several old royal suites, the Terem Palace, the Golden Chamber of the czarina, nine churches dating from the 15th, 16th and 17th centuries, and over 700 separate rooms. The west building housed state reception rooms and the imperial family's private apartments. The noted Russian architect Konstantin Ton, Academician of Architecture and Nicholas I's favourite architect, projected and supervised the building. He was the founder of the eclectic "Russian-Byzantine style" which was officially promoted in Russia at the time. In addition to the Grand Kremlin Palace and the Armoury in the Moscow Kremlin, he also designed the famous Moscow Church of Christ Our Saviour.

The buildings of the palace form a rectangle enclosing an inner courtyard. Its main, south facade faces the Moskva River. Because of its three rows of windows and substantial height (about 47 metres), the palace appears to be three storeys high, but in fact there are only two, for the windows of the top floor are set in two tiers.

The grand entrance to the palace is in the centre of the south

*The Georgievsky Hall
in the Grand Kremlin Palace*

**Carved gilded doors of the Holy Vestibule
which connect the Palace of Facets
with the Vladimirsky Hall**

façade. From the vestibule decorated with granite columns the grand staircase leads to the second floor with an enfilade of vast halls each of which was dedicated to one of the major Russian orders of the period.

High gilt doors open into a splendid grand hall decorated with hollow zinc columns and brightly lit with thousands of lights of great chandeliers reflected in a parquet floor beautifully patterned from twenty kinds of fine wood. This is the Georgievsky (St. George) Hall, named after the Order of St. George, the highest Russian military decoration. There are 1,250 square metres of floor in this 17.5 metre high hall. In the tall niches along the walls are marble slabs engraved in gold with the names of units that distinguished themselves in battle, and of officers and men awarded the Order of St. George. Among them are the names of the famous Russian army and navy commanders such as Field Marshals Suvorov and Kutuzov, Admiral Nakhimov, and others. The marble slabs are divided by beautiful convoluted columns, each crowned with an allegorical statue of a woman holding a laurel wreath in her hands, personifying the victories scored by Russian arms.

The Georgievsky Hall is used for state and diplomatic receptions and official ceremonies such as the presentation of

*The Vladimirsky Hall
in the Grand Kremlin Palace*

*The dome of the Vladimirsky Hall.
Detail*

The Grand Drawing Room ▶

governmental awards and state prizes. After the Victory parade
in 1945 the participants attended a reception held in this hall.
It was also here that Yuri Gagarin, the first man to orbit the
Earth in space, received his Gold Star of Hero of the Soviet
Union in 1961.
Mirror doors lead from the Georgievsky to the octagonal
Vladimirsky (St. Vladimir) Hall, located on the site of the ancient Boyar Square of the Terem Palace. The most impressive
feature of this hall is its steep dome decorated with gilt stucco
moulding. The dome has a skylight from the middle of which
hangs a massive three-tiered chandelier. The Vladimirsky Hall
leads to the palace's older structures — the Palace of Facets,
the czarina's Golden Chamber and the Terem Palace — as well
as into the Winter Garden and the Palace of Congresses.

Top and opposite: Interiors of the Private Chambers (private apartments of the czar's family). Bottom: Part of the Grand Drawing Room

In Soviet times, two halls of the Grand Kremlin Palace, the Alexandrovsky (St. Alexander) and Andreyevsky (St. Andrew) Halls, were combined into one to make the Supreme Soviet Conference Hall. In the past, the Supreme Soviets of the USSR and of the Russian Federation met here for their sessions while today those of the Supreme Soviet of the Russian Federation are held here.

On the ground floor of the Grand Kremlin Palace are the Private Chambers — the imperial family's private apartments — which are carefully preserved as a museum piece. All the rooms are sumptuously decorated with marble, stucco moulding and murals and furnished with expensive furniture demonstrative of the superb skill of the Russian craftsmen. In the Catherine Hall, malachite pilasters made by masters from the Urals are to be seen. And the mantelpiece is faced with small pieces of malachite matched in colour and pattern so skilfully that it seems to be made from a monolith.

THE TEREM PALACE

In 1635-1636, Russian master builders Bazhen Ogurtsov, Antip Konstantinov, Trefil Sharutin and Larion Ushakov built new chambers for the czar on to the parts of the older palace erected by the architect Alevisio Fryazin in 1499-1508. The upper tiers of the palace recede from the lower ones, creating a stepped silhouette and forming open platforms — promenades. The checkered roof glitters in the sun. The carved white-stone frames of the windows, the entrance portals, the cornices decorated with multicoloured tiles, and the parapets of the promenades and staircases lend an especially festive look to the façades.

The Terem Palace helps one form an idea of everyday life in the palace at the time. The old basement built by Alevisio housed service facilities, as well as storerooms and cellars. Part of the Terem Palace was occupied by palatial workshops where ceremonial vestments, clothes and linens for the czar and his family were made and kept. The Czar's living quarters, the Terems, occupied three upper stories. Adjoining them on their south side was a vast open place known as the Boyar Square. From here, a stairway led to the Upper Saviour Square, the

entrance to which was screened off by the famous Golden Grille, skilfully forged from iron, painted and gilded.

The statues of lions supporting gilt shields, behind the Golden Grille, are guarding a white-stone staircase adorned with carved ornamentation. This is the Upper Golden Porch noted for its lavish decoration. A festive looking lacelike stone portal forms the grand entrance to the czar's chambers with low vaulted ceilings, each having three windows.

On entering the palace the first room you walk into is the Front Hall or Anteroom, where boyars gathered in the morning waiting for the czar to appear. The second room, which is called the Cross or Reception Chamber, was where the czar held his conferences. The third chamber, the red-and-gold Throne Room, served as the czar's study. If you take a close look at the façade of the palace, you will see that the middle window of the upper storey, in the czar's study, is decorated with a particularly attractive white-stone surround. It was called the Petition Window for from here a box was lowered into which anyone could put a petition which the czar himself supposedly read and considered. Petitions would lie in wait for a long time and the box came to be known as the Long Box among the common people and gave rise to the saying, "to leave one's business to the Long Box". Next in turn after the Throne Room are the Royal Bedchamber and the Prayer Room.

On the flat roof of the palace stands the Teremok (Small Terem) with a narrow winding staircase leading to it from the Throne Room. The Teremok served no special purpose.

The Terem Palace includes a group of churches: the Upper Cathedral of the Saviour, which was the domestic chapel of the male members of the czar's family, the Church of St. Catherine, the private chapel of the czarinas and the princesses, the Church of the Nativity of Lazarus, the oldest among the Kremlin churches still extant (1393), and several others. In 1680-1681 all these churches were united by a single cornice and roof, crowned with eleven elegant cupolas on slender drums faced in coloured tiles.

Today the only way to enter the Terem Palace is from the Vladimirsky Hall of the Grand Kremlin Palace. The czarina's Golden Chamber, which was part of the former palace of Ivan the Terrible, is half a century older than the Terems. This small room with low vaults and arches covered with paintings on a gold ground, built in the late 16th century, was the official reception room of the czarinas.

A bird's eye view of the Terem Palace

Part of the Throne Hall in the Terem Palace

THE PATRIARCH'S PALACE AND THE CATHEDRAL OF THE TWELVE APOSTLES

Near the Cathedral of the Dormition is the Patriarch's Court with the small five-domed Cathedral of the Twelve Apostles, an architectural monument of the mid-17th century. The ensemble of the Patriarch's Court developed from the Metropolitan's estate founded here early in the 14th century. In 1589, the Metropolitan's Court became the Patriarch's Court when Patriarch Iov, the first Patriarch of Moscow and All Russia, took up residence here. Subsequently Patriarch Filaret, the father of czar Mikhail Fyodorovich Romanov, and Patriarch Nikon, whose aim was to assert the domination of the church over the state, also lived here. It was on the orders of Patriarch Nikon that the Cathedral of the Twelve Apostles, which also served as the grand entrance to the Patriarch's Court, was built in 1652-1656.

The three-storeyed Patriarch's Palace was no less luxurious than the czar's and consisted of many chambers and churches linked by staircases and passageways. Several of its living and service rooms have been preserved together with the cathedral and the main part of the palace, the huge Krestovaya (Cross) Chamber, also known as the Chrism Chamber, with a floor area of 280 square metres and walls 2.35 metres thick.

The well-known 17th-century traveller, Paul of Aleppo, left the following description of the chamber: "Particularly remarkable is its wide vault without central support. Along the perimeter of the chamber steps are made and its floor looks like a pool which has only to be filled with water. It is laid with beautiful coloured tiles. The huge windows look out on to the cathedral (Cathedral of the Dormition — Ed.) and contain small windows fashioned from a wonderful mica and ornamented with seemingly real flowers... Near the door is a huge stove of fine tiles".

In the Krestovaya Chamber a museum of 17th-century applied art and everyday life has been opened, with an exhibition of crystal, glass and embossed plate and of fabrics woven 300 years ago. There is also an exhibition of 17th-century Russian dress. The interior of one of the Patriarch's seven **prikaz** (offices) with a large table and a bench covered with thick cloth, on which clerks used to sit, offers a vivid picture of the distant past. On the table there is a lidded inkpot, sharpened goose quills, parchment scrolls, and books in heavy leather bindings.

The original layout and décor of the Cathedral of the Twelve Apostles have also been largely restored. The two arched gates through which processions once entered the Patriarch's Court from Cathedral Square and which were walled up in the 18th century have been opened.

THE BELL TOWER OF IVAN THE GREAT

Rising high above the architectural ensemble of Cathedral Square and the whole of the Kremlin is the Bell Tower of Ivan the Great. It provides a good view of the surrounding area for 24 to 30 kilometres around. This 81-metre bell tower with a gilt dome represents a magnificent example of 16th-century architecture. The lower tiers were erected by Bon Fryazin in 1505-1508. In 1600, during the reign of czar Boris Godunov, a further two tiers were added supposedly by master builder Fyodor Kon, who embellished the upper part of the drum with a gilt inscription in three rows telling about the event.

The Bell Tower of Ivan the Great with its staircase of 329 steps was for a long time the tallest structure in Moscow. Besides, the pyramidal foundation goes 10 metres beneath the surface of the ground. When retreating from Moscow in 1812, Napoleon ordered the Bell Tower of Ivan the Great to be blown up, but the magnificent structure withstood the blast and only the contiguous belfries were destroyed. In 1814-1815, the entire ensemble was restored. The biggest bell on the belfry, the Dormition Bell, weighs 65,320 kg.

THE CZAR BELL AND THE CZAR CANNON

Beside the Bell Tower of Ivan the Great stands the famous Czar Bell weighing over 200 tons. There is no other metal bell of this size anywhere in the world. It is 6.14 metres high and 6.6 metres in diameter. The complicated job of casting this enormous bell was performed by a team of nearly 200 craftsmen under the supervision of Ivan Motorin and his son Mikhail. During the great fire of 1737 the bell still lay in its casting pile. Because of uneven cooling, which resulted from

The Czar Bell and the Czar Cannon

◀*The Bell Tower of Ivan the Great*

the attempts to extinguish the fire, the red-hot bronze of the bell cracked and a chunk weighing 11.5 tons broke off. After that the Czar Bell remained in the earth for almost 100 years. It was not until 1836 that architect Auguste Montferrand raised it and put it on a granite pedestal. The surface of the bell is finely worked in relief with decorative patterns, embossed pictures, and inscriptions.

The Czar Cannon is another fine example of the craftsmanship of Russian foundrymen. Cast by master Andrei Chokhov in 1586, it is older than the Czar Bell. The cannon weighs 40 tons, is over 5 metres long and has a calibre of 890 mm. The gun carriage and the cannonballs lying nearby are decorative, for the cannon itself was designed to fire not cannonballs but grapeshot.

THE ARMOURY

The State Armoury is the oldest Russian museum. It contains priceless monuments of Russian and foreign applied art that were witnesses of major events in the history of the Russian state and Russian culture.

Reference to the Armoury goes back to 1547. It then consisted of workshops for the manufacture, storage and purchase of combat and dress weapons and armour and articles used in the palace. Gold- and silversmiths, artists, icon-painters, book-painters and decorators, masters of **basma** (a technique in which a pattern is stamped by hand onto a thin plate of gold or silver), enamellers, builders, and many others worked there. Apprentices were also trained in the various crafts. Highly artistic gold and silver plate for use in the palace and for royal grants, jewellery, richly decorated harnesses, gold-embroidered banners and icons were all produced.

The Armoury reached its heyday in 1650-1670 when Boyar Bogdan Khitrovo was in charge of the Kremlin workshops to which he called the finest Russian masters of various crafts and skilful craftsmen from the West and the East. In 1700, the valuable objects, which had been kept in the Czar's Gold and Silver Chambers went to join the collection in the Armoury which thus became the richest treasury in the country.

After Peter the Great transferred most craftsmen to St. Petersburg in 1711, production fell off in the workshops of the Armoury, which may well be regarded as a 17th-century Russian Academy of Arts. The Armoury became mostly a repository and was converted into a museum in 1806.

The present-day structure of the Armoury near the Borovitsky Gate was built in 1844-1851 by the architect Konstantin Ton. He fused the two buildings, the old and the new, into a single ensemble. The high vaulted halls of the second storey with two tiers of windows form an enfilade with a round hall in the middle and two semicircular halls at the sides. On the walls of the halls are 58 marble medallions with portraits of Russian princes and czars, produced by the outstanding Russian sculptor Fedot Shubin in 1774-1775.

The art treasures collected in the Armoury are of world significance. Each article is distinguished by great beauty and perfection of form and demonstrates the exceptional skill of the craftsmen who made it. The Armoury's riches are absolutely unique.

Here is a cup which Prince Yuri Dolgoruky, the founder of Moscow, once held in his hands. Here is the famous Cap of Monomachus, the crown of the Russian grand princes and

The Armoury collection:
helmet; armour

The Armoury collection: gold dipper; the diamond throne of czar Alexei Mikhailovich

czars. Legend has it that this sable-trimmed head-dress decorated with precious stones and topped by a pearl-tipped gold cross, supposedly made in Central Asia in the 13th-14th centuries, was sent by Emperor Constantine Monomachus of Byzantium to his grandson, Grand Prince Vladimir Monomachus of Kiev. It also crowned the head of Ivan the Terrible in his day. It was only in 1721 that an imperial crown began to be used for the coronation of the Russian czars, and the cap has since been kept as a precious relic.

Here is the ivory staff on which Ivan the Terrible leaned. Here are the high boots which Peter the Great was wearing when he chose the site for the future Northern capital, St. Petersburg. Here is the banner under which Cossack Ataman Yermak Timofeyevich came to Siberia...

Arms, armour and military attributes of the 13th-18th centuries, exquisite works by 12th-19th century gold- and silversmiths and the world's most complete collection of 14th-19th century clothing and fabrics are all to be seen in the halls of the Armoury.

Among the gifts to the Russian czars from various countries of the West and the East are works by Polish, German, English,

Dutch, and French jewellers of the 15th-19th centuries and art objects made of crystal, jasper and carved ivory.

On show are such exceptionally valuable works of 13th-17th century art as gold coronets, crowns, sceptres and orbs adorned with precious stones, as well as ancient thrones, including the throne of Ivan the Terrible, covered with relief ivory carvings, and the diamond throne of czar Alexei Mikhailovich, made by Armenian craftsmen in Iran.

Two halls of the Armoury contain samples of dress harnesses made by Russian and foreign craftsmen, which used to be kept in the palace's Equestrian Section. Especially splendid are saddles, horse-cloths and bridles from Oriental countries, decorated with gold and precious stones. The last or ninth hall contains a unique collection of carriages.

The Armoury collection: ceremonial saddle (top, left); ceremonial attire of czar Mikhail Romanov: crown, orb and sceptre (bottom); embroidery in pearls and precious stones. 17th century (opposite)

THE DIAMOND FUND EXHIBITION

A kind of continuation of the Armoury display is the USSR Diamond Fund Exhibition housed in the same building, which was opened in 1967. Here on display is part of the Soviet Union's diamond treasury. The exhibits include the great imperial crown of gold, silver, diamonds and pearls made for the coronation of Empress Catherine II, a sceptre and orb covered with diamonds, the world's largest Ceylon sapphire (258.8 carats), the legendary giant diamonds **Orlov** (189.6 carats) and **Shah** (88.7 carats), and the largest gold nugget to have been preserved in the world, weighing 36 kg.

The pieces of 18th-19th century jewellery which are to be seen here are truly inimitable. Also to be seen are pieces of modern jewellery by Soviet masters, which are no less beautiful than the masterpieces of the past. Also on view are the finest diamonds found in Yakutia such as **Oktyabrsky, Komsomolsky, Golden Prague, The Great Beginning,** and the 232-carat **Star of Yakutia,** the largest diamond found in the Soviet Union so far, as well as are gold nuggets, including **Mephistopheles,** which seems to be a sculpture created by Nature herself.

The Diamond Fund treasures: the Great Brooch; the Orlov Diamond; the Grand Bouquet ornament (opposite)

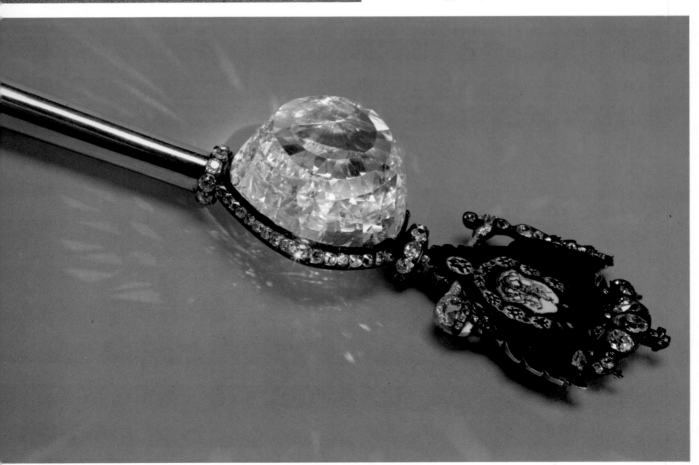

Church of St. Barbara in Varvarka Street.
1796-1801. Architect R. Kazakov

THE KITAIGOROD

Archeological excavations show that a settlement existed on the site of the present-day Kitaigorod even before Moscow was first mentioned in the chronicles. This is corroborated by the articles of domestic use, clothing, ornaments, remains of ancient craftsmen's workshops, and foundations of buildings dating from the 11th century that have been unearthed here. The establishment of a **posad,** or trading quarter, near the walls of a citadel is a phenomenon typical of the history of European cities. The posad on the Moskva River near its confluence with the Yauza River had its own landing stage and its own warehouses. It grew rapidly and soon began to be called Veliky Posad (Great Trading Quarter). As a result of its advantageous location where waterways and surface roads crossed it became a permanent mart, a centre of exchange of goods between the East and the West and between the South and the North.

Fragments of the old Kitaigorod wall can still be seen in Sverdlov Square behind the Metropol Hotel and in Kitai Passage in front of one of the façades of the Rossiya Hotel.

RAZIN STREET

Razin Street was given its present name in the postrevolutionary period in honour of Don Cossack Stepan Razin, leader of the peasant revolt against feudal oppression in the 17th century, hero of numerous folk songs and legends. It was along this street that on June 6, 1671, he was led to execution in Red Square. Mention of the street itself dates back to as early as the 14th century. Tradition has it that in 1380 the Russian army led by Dmitri Donskoi passed along this very street (which once began at the Timofeyevskaya Tower of the Kremlin, where the Konstantino-Yeleninskaya Tower was later built) on its way to fight the famous Kulikovo Battle. From the very beginning, the principal residents were "guests from overseas"— rich foreign merchants who acted as Moscow's intermediaries in international trade. The manors of ancient boyar families also stood here. By the mid-15th century the street took on its present aspect and in the 16th century it was named Varvarka after the Church of St. Barbara standing at the entrance. Today former Varvarka Street is a veritable open-air museum of Russian architecture with a number of rare exhibits.

THE OLD ENGLISH COURT

The Old English Court, a monument of 16th-17th century architecture, is one of the oldest civil structures in Moscow to have survived to this day. The original building, whose lower, white-stone storey has been preserved, dates from the early 16th century.

In 1555, soon after the first English-Russian trade agreement was concluded, Ivan the Terrible granted the court to the English. As the volume of English-Russian trade grew, the English bought still other property in Moscow and their court in Varvarka came to be known as the Old English Court.

The Old English Court was neither a residential building nor a palace: it fully conformed to its purpose of being the main English residence in Moscow. On the first floor of the building was the formal reception room, the Official Chamber. The rooms of the ground floor, isolated from one another, were used as storerooms, cellars, and pantries. The high attic served for storing wares.

In 1649, in accordance with the czar's ukase, the English left Russia. The estate together with the house and all the outbuildings was sold to Boyar I.A. Miloslavsky. In 1669, the estate was turned over to the Ambassadorial Office and in 1676 the Moscow residence of the Metropolitan of Nizhni Novgorod was established here. In the reign of Peter the Great, the building housed the school of Mathematics.

The building acquired its present-day appearance after restoration work of 1969-1972 which cleared away later additions.

The Old English Court in Varvarka Street.
16th-17th centuries

*View of the Balchug-Kempinski Hotel
and the Rossiya Hotel (left)*

The Trinity Church in Nikitniki ▶

THE TRINITY CHURCH IN NIKITNIKI

In Nikitnikov Lane near Razin Street stands one of the most beautiful old churches in Moscow, the Trinity Church in Nikitniki, also known as the Church of the Georgian Icon of Our Lady. Built by the merchant Grigori Nikitnikov on his own estate, it also served as a parish church. Nikitnikov was so wealthy that he not infrequently lent money to the czar himself and he spared no expense in building the church, all the more so as the south chapel, the Chapel of St. Nicetas the Warrior, became the family burial place.

The church is considered the finest example of 17th-century Russian ornamental architecture. It is remarkable for its wealth of decorative ornamentation, particularly the beautiful **kokoshniki** (an architectural element in the form of a Russian woman's headdress) around the elegant gilt cupolas, and the complex spatial composition in the traditions of old-time Rus-

sian house-building. Not by chance was it dubbed an encyclopedia of the architectural techniques which were later used in many of the buildings in Moscow of the time.

The walls in the church are covered with frescoes by the "royal masters" of the Armoury such as Simon Ushakov, Yakov Kazanets, Osip Vladimirov, and others, and they have remained in an excellent state of preservation. The iconostasis of the main church was executed by Moscow and Yaroslavl carvers. Scenes from the Apocalypse painted on the walls of the side Chapel of St. John the Evangelist, which is under the belfry, stand out for their unconventional treatment of the subject. In 1904, still another private chapel, dedicated to the Georgian Icon of Our Lady which had been in the church since 1653, was set up in the basement.

The Polytechnic Museum. 1847-77,
architect I. Monighetti; 1896,
architect N. Shokhin; 1907,
architects P. Voyeikov
and V. Yerameshantsev

The City Duma. 1890-92,
architect D. Chichagov

The building of Moscow Mayor's ▶
Office in Tverskaya Street

The Loan Office building. ▶
1913-16, architects V. Pokrovsky
and B. Nilus

Triumphalnaya Square at night

Opposite, top: the National Hotel. 1903, ▶
architect A. Ivanov; bottom:
the Belorussia Railway Station

THE BOLSHOI THEATRE

This old square lies in the very centre of the radial-circular network of Moscow streets. It took shape in 1817 after the Neglinnaya River was piped underground and the hilly and marshy area was drained and levelled. At the time the entire perimeter of the square, which was then called Petrovskaya Square, was built up with symmetrically situated two-storeyed buildings whose façades were designed in the same style. In 1824, a new building of the Bolshoi (Petrovsky) Theatre was erected in place of the old one which had burnt down. The inner part of the square was an empty unpaved area, fenced off by thick ropes, which was intended for military reviews and parades.

This strictly symmetrical ensemble in the neoclassical style was designed by the noted architect Osip Beauvais. The only still extant example of the buildings that originally stood around the square is the Maly Theatre erected in 1821. In 1830 the square was renamed Teatralnaya (Theatre) Square and it was given its present name in 1919.

In the northern part of the square stands the Bolshoi Theatre with a monumental colonnade and quadriga of bronze horses on its pediment, which has become one of the symbols of Moscow. Built in 1820-1824 to the design of architects Alexander Mikhailov and Osip Beauvais, it is one of the finest theatre buildings in the world, a monumental work of 19th-century Russian neoclassicism. In 1855-1856, after a fire, it was in great part rebuilt by the architect Albert Kavos, who preserved its original general layout but increased the height of the building, added a third storey, and put up a gallery supported by iron columns on either side of the building. The five-tiered auditorium is famous for its excellent acoustics and rich ornamentation. A splendid great crystal chandelier hangs from the ceiling which is decorated with a painting. The auditorium, seating 2,153, is 21 metres high, 25 metres long and 26 metres wide.

Quite a few outstanding artists have performed on the stage of the Bolshoi. Fyodor Chaliapin sang here and Galina Ulanova and Maya Plisetskaya danced on its boards. Today a younger generation of fine Soviet performers are keeping up the worldwide fame of the Bolshoi Theatre.

THE HALL OF COLUMNS
OF THE TRADE UNION HOUSE

The Hall of Columns of the Trade Union House is a pearl of neoclassical architecture. The masterpiece was created by M.F. Kazakov. In the 1760s he was commissioned by Prince V.M. Dolgorukov-Krymsky, the Governor-General of Moscow, to re-build an old structure at the corner of Bolshaya Dmitrovka Street (now Pushkinskaya). The new building, which incorporated part of the older one, was then purchased by Moscow nobility and used as a social centre. Since then, the Hall has been the scene of gala functions and concerts given in celebration of festive occasions. The guests included Pushkin and Lermontov, Tchaikovsky and Rimsky-Korsakov, Rachmaninov and Liszt. Prominent musicians considered it a privilege to perform in that famous Hall.

Nowadays, the Hall is Moscow's No. l concert and conference hall. The Moscow Patriarchy, for instance, held a meeting there to celebrate the Millenium of Baptism in Russia.

The acoustics of the Hall are excellent, the credit for which goes to the architect, Kazakov, but this is not, of course, its only attraction. The Hall's appeal lies chiefly in its unique architecture. In choosing the means of expression, the architect succeeded in finding the tenuous line that distinguishes the simplicity of perfection from near-asceticism.

The old building of Moscow University.
1786-93, architect M. Kazakov

MOSCOW UNIVERSITY

In 1714, Peter the Great promulgated a ukase prohibiting the construction of stone buildings in Moscow. This was explained by an acute shortage of stonemasons, who were needed for building the new Russian capital. At the time St. Petersburg had the appearance of a modern European city, whereas Moscow retained all the features of Old Russian architecture. It was not until the 1780s that the ancient Russian capital began to be developed on a vast scale once again. This was a new period in the history of Russian architecture and its main proponent in Moscow was Matvei Kazakov, who built a number of structures which largely determined the new look of the city. It is no accident that the period of neoclassicism in Russian architecture is often called the Kazakov period.

Moscow University, erected in 1786-1793, had all the principal characteristic features of neoclassicism. It was one of the largest structures of the period in Moscow. The fire of 1812, however, did not spare the university and for several years the black ruins of this once magnificent building remained untouched.

Restoration began in 1817. The famous architect Domenico Gilardi was commissioned to do the job and two years later he successfully completed reconstruction. The talented successor of Kazakov, however, departed from the original design in many respects and introduced his own principles into the reconstruction work, favouring the Empire style.

The assembly hall of Moscow University has come down to us in a good state of preservation. Here one can see a "Kazakovian" light colonnade with a choir along the semicircular wall, and also a ceiling painting executed from sketches by Gilardi, who was a superb graphic artist. The stucco moulding decorating the building is the work of I. Yemelyanov and I. Meshkov. The bas-relief **Triumph of Sciences and Arts** which is to be seen behind the columns of the central portico, the emblem on the pediment and the lion masks above the first-floor windows were executed by G.T. Zamarayev.

Today Moscow University, a building embodying the conceptions of various talented artists and architects, remains a remarkable monument of Russian architecture adorning the centre of Moscow.

BOROVITSKAYA SQUARE.
THE PASHKOV HOUSE

On the crest of the hill opposite the Borovitsky Gate of the Kremlin stands the Pashkov House, one of the most beautiful buildings in Moscow. The house was built in 1784-1786 by the famous Russian architect Vasili Bazhenov, but it is better known by the name of its first owner Pashkov, a rich Moscow nobleman.

The main building itself and the wings connected to it by galleries, combined into a single harmonious whole, betray a rare sense of proportion. The pleasing perfection of the building and the beauty of its decoration arouse the admiration of everyone who sees it. No less beautiful is the inner courtyard with the main gate.

The Pashkovs did not own the house for long. As early as 1839 it was sold to the Treasury and from 1862 it housed the Rumyantsev Museum and Public Library.

Count Nikolai Rumyantsev (1754-1826) was an eminent Russian statesman and diplomat and a well-known collector of Russian antiques, manuscripts, books and works of art. As stipulated in his will, when he died all his rich collections were turned over to the state.

The Pashkov House in Borovitskaya Square.
1786, architect V. Bazhenov

THE A.S. PUSHKIN MUSEUM OF FINE ARTS

Exterior. The idea of establishing a Museum of foreign art in Moscow emerged way back at the beginning of the 19th century. The progressive intelligentsia nurtured it for a long time. An extensive public movement to raise funds for the construction of such a museum arose in Moscow. Donations varied from a copeck to thousands of rubles.

Professor I.V. Tsvetayev of Moscow University, a leading expert in ancient philology and art, the father of the famous poetess M.I. Tsvetayeva, was the moving spirit of this noble project. Incidentally, he was the first director of the Museum. The building was designed by R.I. Klein who was made an academician of architecture after construction work had been completed.

The Museum took from 1898 to 1912 to build. Initially called the Fine Arts Museum, it got its present name in 1937.

The Museum building is classicist in style. The elongated façade with an Ionic colonnade on both sides forming two deep loggias, the protruding portico with a stairway ascending to it at a gently sloping angle impart to the building, for all its seeming bulk, extraordinary lightness, even grace. This impression is enhanced by a low fence with neat lawns behind it.

The names of the founders of the Museum have been perpetuated by memorial plaques.

A broad stairway by the architect I. Zholtovsky leads from the front entrance to the Museum. Made of artificial and natural marble, the stairway is flanked with slender columns.

At first, the Museum's collection was rathed modest. It had on display plaster copies of ancient, medieval and Renaissance sculptures, and only a few originals: nine paintings by various artists, a set of Egyptian antiques, Greek vases, Italian paintings of the 14th-16th centuries, bronze articles from France of the 18th and the early 19th centuries.

After the October 1917 Revolution, priceless treasures of Western European culture from the former Rumyantsev Museum, the Hermitage and the Tretyakov Gallery and from nationalized private collections were handed over to the Museum.

Today the Museum has about 3,000 paintings, 250,000 drawings and engravings, 100,000 coins and medals, and a large number of works of applied art. This rich collection represents a period from antiquity right to the present day. We shall dwell here only on some of the works of art of display in the Museum.

PERUGINO. Pictures dating back to the early 15th century and the so-called High Renaissance (the late 15th and the first half of the 16th centuries) periods are to be seen in the halls given over to Italian art of the 15th-16th centuries. Pietro Vannucci (Perugino), the teacher of great Raphael, was among the initiators of new art which concentrated on the beauty of the real world and of man, with all his passions, weaknesses and sins, and with his spiritual quests.

The Museum boasts a Perugino masterpiece, **The Madonna and Child.**

REMBRANDT. The greatest painter of the 17th-century Dutch school, Rembrandt van Rijn, is represented in the Museum by six pictures belonging to various periods of his work. He was mainly concerned with historical and Biblical subjects, which did not at all mean that the artist had distanced himself from the life around him. These subjects enabled Rembrandt to combine harsh reality with sublimity, to convey the psychological state of his heroes in dramatic moments and the whole gamut of human passions.

One of the most famous Rembrandt paintings, **Ahasuerus, Haman and Esther,** displayed in the Museum, is typical in this respect. It illustrates the well-known story of Esther, the Jewish wife of the Persian King Ahasuerus, as she tells her husband about the perfidious plans of Haman, his vizier and friend, who is scheming to destroy her people. The Biblical parable was used by Rembrandt as a pretext to show a clash of destinies and characters. The picture depicts the culminating moment: Esther has just exposed Haman. The dark brown background with flaming dark red hues stresses the drama of the situation, the depressed state of the personages who are about to make a crucial decision. The King and his wife sit side by side, with Haman standing well away from them. The composition of the picture suggests a barrier of estrangement between former friends. The vizier's posture implies that he

Madonna and Child. 15th century. By Perugino

Ahasuerus, Haman and Esther. 17th century.
By Rembrandt van Rijn

knows full well what he is in for but hasn't abandoned all hope yet. The King is also tense. As for Esther, she looks all gentleness, devotion and tenderness in her golden-coloured brocade dress. The impression is further enhanced by gleams of light playing on her face. In general, the play of light and shade, brought to perfection by Rembrandt, is used by the artist as a means of saturating his canvases with emotion.

DEGAS. French art of the second half of the 19th century is represented in the Museum by magnificent impressionist paintings. Edgar Degas emphasizes prosaic, petty but very characteristic features of his personages' life. The pictures **Dancers in Rehearsal, A Dancer Sitting for a Photograph** and **Blue Dancers** are cases in point.

The picture **A Dancer Sitting for a Photograph** is done in grey and blue. The woman tries to strike a coquettish pose, but the artist discerns in this movement the angular awkwardness of a tired woman. She will be gracefulness itself in a moment, but we know how much effort it will cost her, and how hard the road to perfection is.

And here are the **Blue Dancers** absorbed in the magic of dance. This is the acme of their art, with exhausting rehearsals behind them, and with an exacting audience looking on. The ease of motion in the whirlwind of colours and lines, and the abandon with which the dancers perform the dance, cannot but cast a spell on the viewer. The harmony of confident brushwork and a warm golden glow with a tinge of blue, the sheer magic of art, impart a tremendous emotional appeal to the picture.

Blue Dancers. 19th century. By Edgar Degas　　　　　　　*The Cathedral of Christ the Redeemer* ▶

The Pushkin Museum in Prechistenka Street
(formely Kropotkinskaya Street). Early 19th century,
architect A. Grigoryev

KROPOTKINSKAYA STREET

Two streets — Kropotkinskaya and Ostozhenka — converge at a sharp angle and marge into Volkhonka, where the majestic Church of Christ the Saviour once stood (now there is a public swimming pool in its place). Both streets, with their infinite variety of architectural styles ranging from provincial whimsy to classical harmony, are relics of old Moscow. Surprisingly, this eclecticism is not at all offensive to the eye; on the contrary it lends these streets a charm all their own. Each house retains the soul which its architect has put into it.

We shall begin our story with the Kropotkinskaya Street (formerly Prechistenka). It owes its old name to a decree of czar Alexei Mikhailovich — the street led to the Church of the Holy Virgin (Prechistaya Bogomater) in the Novodevichy Convent.

Prechistenka is a legacy of the Moscow of the epoch of neoclassicism, the Moscow of Pushkin, the Moscow of the Decembrists. It is sometimes referred to, with good reason, as a museum of Russian architecture of the early 19th century. However, the first recorded mention of it goes back to the 16th century. At that time czar Ivan the Terrible's henchmen and soldiers settled there, and the street abounded in pubs, taverns and small shops selling flour and pancakes, for the most part. Ancient structures are still being unearthed in Kropotkinskaya Street, named after Prince Kropotkin, the noted revolutionary anarchist, scientist and traveller, in 1921. Quite recently, restorers found ancient masonry and heavy vaults behind the plastered walls of No. 1, an ordinary-looking house standing at the point where Ostozhenka and Kropotkinskaya meet. It turned out that the house enclosed a fine specimen of 17th-century Russian architecture, the residence of the Golovins, an aristocratic family. Next to it (No. 1/2), a beautiful white-stone mansion of the Lopukhins' estate was dug out from later "cultural strata". Both buildings, restored to their original appearance, have been handed over to the USSR Book Chamber. The stone house of the nobleman F. Saltykov, a son-in-law of czar Ivan Alexeyevich, has survived in a Kropotkinskaya by-street since the 17th century.

The buildings created at the end of the 18th century by the famous Russian architect M.F. Kazakov have lost none of their eye-appeal. This is true, first and foremost, of the palace in

House No. 17 belonged to the father of the Decembrist I.G. Bibikov, a member of the "Union for Prosperity". One day, Pushkin was invited to a ball here. The poet often called on his friends who lived in Kropotkinskaya. Incidentally, No. 17 was later bought by Denis Davydov, the legendary partisan and poet. The other Decembrists who lived in that street included M.F. Orlov (at No. 10), N.V. Vsevolzhsky, A.P. Vyazemsky, A.A. Tuchkov.

Practically every house in the former Prechistenka is a unique specimen of Russian architecture associated with the famous men of the past.

In 1921, the famous American dancer Isadora Duncan took up her residence in No. 20, a two-storey mansion, and opened her Free Dance Studio there. When he married her, the great Russian poet Sergei Yesenin also moved in. No. 32 used to be the well-known secondary school run by L. Polivanov, to which the poets V. Bryusov, A. Bely and M. Voloshin went. Kropotkinskaya recalls the great painters M. Vrubel, V. Serov, V. Surikov, I. Levitan who lived and worked there.

A street of poets, artists and progressive public figures, it has inscribed a vivid page in the history of Moscow.

Portrait of Alexander Pushkin by P. Sokolov

Part of a young gentleman's study. 1830s

neoclassical style which belonged to the Princes Dolgoruky (No. 19). Restored after the 1812 fire, it changed its appearance slightly, but kept its charm. Along with his disciples, Kazakov designed the Prechistenskaya police station complete with fire brigade quarters (No. 22). A.I. Herzen was kept in custody there for a while.

Unique examples of 19th-century architecture also catch the eye. Outstanding among them is No. 12, the former town estate of the Khrushchevs-Seleznevs, built to a design by the architect A.G. Grigoryev. Its splendour is set off to the best advantage by the central and side façades with their delicately columned porticoes. The State Pushkin Museum was opened there in 1961.

House No. 11 has to do with another great Russian writer — it is the Lev Tolstoy Museum. This building in Empire style is also by the architect Grigoryev. Paintings by famous masters such as Repin, Kramskoi, Nesterov and Ghe are on display there. The visitors can hear the voice of Lev Tolstoy as recorded on the phonograph the inventor Edison presented to the writer.

Kekusheva's mansion in Ostozhenka Street.
1900-01, architect L. Kekushev

OSTOZHENKA

Only recently has its historical name been restored to Osto-zhenka. In 1935 it was renamed Metrostroyevskaya in honour of the builders of Moscow's first metro route which stretched from the Recreation Park to Sokolniki.

In the 17th century, vast hay fields clothed the sloping banks of the Moscow river, and what is now the middle of the street was a suburb called Konyushenny which gave its name to one of the nearby lanes (Starokonyushenny).

Earlier still, in the 14th century, the Alexeyevsky Convent stood there. After a fire, it was transferred first to the Kremlin and then to Chertolye. In 1584, the Zachatyevsky Convent was built on the site by the wish of czar Fyodor Ivanovich and czarina Irina. The later buildings, dating to the 17th-18th centuries, have survived to this day.

Just like the neighbouring Prechistenka, Ostozhenka was favoured by the nobility which started settling there in the times of Ivan the Terrible. The names of the local noble residents live on in the names of the lanes branching off the street — Tur-chaninov, Khilkov, Lopukhinsky, Yeropkinsky, and others.

Post-revolutionary reconstruction left Ostozhenka practically intact, and many structures of Russian classicistic architecture have survived there since the 18th-19th centuries. One of the most beautiful among them is the house on the estate of General-in-Chief P.D. Yeropkin built in 1771 (No. 38), with its fantastic colonnade. At the beginning of the 19th century, the house was purchased by Moscow merchants who transferred their business school there. The well-known Russian historian S.M. Solovyov and the writer I.A. Goncharov, the author of the novels **Oblomov, The Chasm, The Same Old Story,** were born in this house. Today it is the Maurice Thorez State Pedagogical Institute of Foreign Languages. In front of the Institute building there is a stele commemorating the volunteers who set out from here for the front lines during the Great Patriotic War and died in action. Right opposite the Institute, there is a small mansion with columns (No. 37), which belonged to the mother of the writer Ivan Turgenev.

At the beginning of the 19th century, a palace in classicist style was built for Grand Duke Mikhail Pavlovich at the end of the street, in place of the 17th-century herdsmen's camp. Right opposite it, in place of the "Czar's Own Stables" (No. 48), food stores were built in 1827. Radically reconstructed three years later, the stores became a fine specimen of Russian Empire architecture. Designed by Academician V. Stasov, the stores were built under the supervision of Academician M. Shestakov.

Many houses in Ostozhenka, like those in Kropotkinskaya, are associated with the names of outstanding personalities of the past: M. Bakunin and P. Nashchokin, V. Belinsky (who lived in Savelevsky lane near Ostozhenka), the singer N. Lavrov, who scintillated on the Moscow stage then.

Church of St. Nicholas in Khamovniki (1679-82), near the Park Kultury Metro Station

THE MOSCOW BOULEVARD RING

The chain of Moscow boulevards is not really a ring at all, but a horseshoe, which encircles the centre and touches the Moskva River on either side. At one time the boundary of Moscow passed here and in 1586-1692 a fortress wall on a white-stone foundation was built along this line. Armed with cannon, it reliably protected the settlements that had grown up outside the limits of the Kremlin and the Kitaigorod from enemy raids. The wall, erected by the noted master builder Fyodor Kon was over 9 kilometres long and 4.5 to 6 metres thick. Where it intersected the radial streets, towers with gates were built.

In the late 18th-early 19th centuries the fortifications had lost their military significance and were taken down. In their place ten boulevards were laid. The boulevards took final shape after the fire of 1812. Squares took the place of the former city gates and many of them have retained their former names: Nikitsky Gate, Petrovsky Gate, Pokrovsky Gate, Yauzsky Gate, etc.

CHISTIYE PRUDY

Chistoprudny Boulevard, or Chistiye Prudy as it is often called, begins at Kirovsky Gate Square and ends at the Pokrovsky Gate where the Boulevard Ring intersects Chernyshevsky Street. The boulevard gets its name from the Chisty (Clear) Pond located almost in its centre. In summer, ducks and swans swimming across the mirrorlike surface of the pond are a pleasing sight and in winter a skating-rink is opened here.

The local ponds were cleared and began to be maintained on the orders of Alexander Menshikov, the famous associate of Peter the Great, from 1703 when he began to construct his manor in the neighbourhood. Today you can still see the Church of St. Gabriel the Archangel, known as Menshikov's Tower, at the end of Telegrafny Lane off Chistiye Prudy.

This remarkably graceful, light, elegant and lavishly decorated tower, which is one of the finest works of early 18th-century Russian architecture, combines the traditions of 17th-century Russian church architecture with the techniques of neoclassical architecture, and was built by the exceptionally talented architect Ivan Zarudny, commissioned by Menshikov, in 1704-1707. The façades of the church are sumptuously decorated with columns and relief white-stone carving.

THE SUVOROV BOULEVARD
WITH A VIEW OF THE LUNIN'S HOUSE

The Suvorov Boulevard is the part of the boulevard ring stretching from the Arbat Square to Nikitskiye Vorota. Originally, the boulevard was called Nikitsky, but renamed Suvorov in 1950 on the occasion of the 150th anniversary of the death of the great Russian marshal. It appeared shortly after the walls of the Bely Gorod (White Town) had been pulled down in the first half of the 19th century.

Particularly striking among the buildings flanking the boulevard is a group of structures at No. 12a, known as the Lunin's House, which belonged to General P.M. Lunin, the uncle of the Decembrist, M.S. Lunin. This masterpiece by the architect D.I. Gilardi is a perfect example of the Empire style of the early 19th century. The group of buildings dates back to 1818-1823.

The buildings have been reconstructed recently, and their exterior and interior decoration restored, to house the State Museum of Oriental Art.

Opposite: Church of St. Gabriel the Archangel (Menshikov's Tower) in Chistiye Prudy. Early 18th century
On this page, top: the Lunins' house in Nikitsky Boulevard (formely the Suvorov Boulevard); bottom: The Shekhtel house

On the next page: The main staircase in the Shekhtel house

THE SHEKHTEL HOUSE
(MAXIM GORKY MUSEUM)

At the end of the 19th century Moscow architecture was marked by a medley of different styles.

Against the background of overall eclecticism, an interesting trend in architecture — "art nouveau" — took shape. The architect F.O. Shekhtel, one of the new style's better-known adherents, designed many buildings in Moscow which was growing rapidly at the time, railway stations, banks, apartment houses, printshops, mansions. His best works include the mansion of the industrialist Ryabushinsky built in 1900-1902.

In designing the Ryabushinsky mansion, Shekhtel departed from the Russian architectural tradition of emphasizing the façade; instead, he arranged the planes in such a way that they added up to a three-dimensional whole.

The interior layout is also governed by new laws. The rooms are not lined up in a habitual suite, but grouped around the front staircase.

Maxim Gorky lived there in the thirties, and later a museum was installed here to commemorate the writer.

The former house of A. Morozov,
factory owner. Late 19th century,
architect V. Mazyrin

On the next pages, left: high-rise administrative building
(former CMEA premises) opposite "The White House";
right, top: The Prague Restaurant at the corner
of New and Old Arbat Streets, and bottom: Church
of St. Simeon the Stylite in New Arbat Street.
Built in 1679, restored in 1968

THE HOUSE OF FRIENDSHIP
IN VOZDVIZHENKA STREET

Moscow architecture of the late 19th-early 20th centuries is extremely varied. At the time, the clients had grown more demanding since Russia's cultural ties with Europe had increased in scope and now most wealthy people had an opportunity to see the architecture of European countries first hand, returning from their travels with ideas on architecture. A highly unusual monument from this period is factory owner A. Morozov's house in Vozdvizhenka Street (now Kalinin Prospekt). While travelling through Europe, Morozov had been enchanted by medieval Spanish architecture and was particularly enraptured by an old Moorish castle. On his return home he launched an unprecedented project when he decided to build a replica of the castle he had loved so much right in the heart of Moscow. Naturally, reproduction of the original turned out to be impossible for a variety of reasons, lack of

space being not the least of them. However, V. Mazyrin, the architect who was commissioned to implement the original conception, did a very good job of it. In 1895-1899, the somewhat shocked Muscovites were given the pleasure of seeing a building that was absolutely foreign to Russian architecture. The fancy turrets, openwork stone lace and huge sea shells on the façade of the structure were the talk of the town at the time.
Morozov's fancy, however, went no further than the outward appearance of the building. On the inside it was a perfectly comfortable dwelling with numerous rooms, beautiful staircases and rich eclectic décor. All this has made it possible to use the mansion in our day as a public building. It is now occupied by the House of Friendship with the Peoples of Foreign Countries.

Old Arbat Street, a favourite haunt of Muscovites and visitors to the city

ARBAT

The street is among those fanning out from the Arbat Square. In times of old, many battles were fought at the intersection of these roads, on close approaches to the Kremlin. It was here that Muscovites rebuffed foreign invaders who had attacked Russia. The square came into being at the end of the 18th century when the last tower of the White Town, with its Arbat Gate, was pulled down. The fire of 1812 reduced to ashes all the structures on the square — as elsewhere in the city — including the wooden theatre of amazing beauty created by the famous architect Carlo Rossi. Nor have many of the buildings erected after the fire come down to us either.

Where does the non-Russian name "Arbat" come from? Experts agree that the street owes its name to Oriental merchants. "Rabad" is Arabic for suburb, and that part of Moscow was just that in the 14th-16th centuries.

Arbat burned many times, was often rebuilt, and took on its final shape at the end of the 18th and the beginning of the 19th centuries. The Russian noble families — the Sheremetevs, Golitsyns, Obolenskys, Ostermans, Bobrinskys — lived there.

After the 1812 fire, Arbat was restored, and the architecture of most of its new buildings was in the Empire style. The mansion of Count Bobrinsky (No. 37) and other structures are among the surviving specimens. Other houses have changed beyond recognition. Khitrovo house (No. 53), in which Pushkin and his young wife, Natalie Goncharova, spent their honeymoon was thoroughly reconstructed. Incidentally, that was the poet's only apartment in Moscow. Before his wedding, Pushkin gave a "stag party" for his friends — the poet Vyazemsky, Yazykov, Baratynsky, Denis Davydov, and others. This house is now a memorial museum.

Muscovites are well acquainted with the massive colonnaded building of the world-famous Vakhtangov Theatre, built in 1947 to a design by the architect P.V. Abrosimov.

The by-streets and lanes branching off Arbat are also associated with many events and famous names. The members of Stankevich's literary philosophical society met in Bolshoi Afanasyevs Lane and had heated discussions there in which Bakunin and Belinsky took part. The gatherings were vividly described by Herzen in his **My Past and Thoughts,** and by Turgenev in his **Rudin.**

The well-known Russian composer A. Skriabin lived at No. 11 in Vakhtangov street. His flat is now a memorial museum. Right across the road are the Shchukin Drama School and the Opera School of the Moscow Conservatoire which have had many celebrities among their graduates. In Krivoarbatsky Lane one can see a unique house by the Moscow architect K. Melnikov known for his ingenuity. In this case, however, he seems to have surpassed himself. The house consists of two upright cylinders, one half-sunk in the other, with a multitude of honeycomb windows. The Spas na Peskakh church in the Spasopeskovsky Lane is a joy to the eye.

Recently, Arbat has been turned into a pedestrian zone of shops, cafes and snack-bars, some of them outdoor. The street has become a popular promenade. Actors and musicians put on amusing shows, artists display their pictures, and poets deliver recitations to appreciative audiences. Arbat with its cosy courtyards has been romanticized by the Soviet bard Bulat Okudzhava, whose wistfully nostalgic and lyrical songs strike a responsive chord in every Muscovite's heart.

Matryoshka dolls, to keep one's
sweet memories
of Russia and Arbat artists

A lovely spot in Arbat

THE CHURCH OF ST. IOANN
THE WARRIOR IN YAKIMANKA

The Church of St. Ioann the Warrior is one of the most interesting monuments of old Moscow. It was built in 1709-1713 when the Moscow baroque was ever more resolutely ousted by new, Petrine architecture. In its appearance the church combines elements characteristic of both these trends of Russian architecture.

In the church stands a carved gilt wooden iconostasis from the Church of the Resurrection in Kadashi. Another remarkable feature of this church is a wrought-iron openwork grille dating to 1754.

Carved gilt wooden iconostasis from the Church of St. Ioann the Warrior

Igumnov's Mansion in Yakimanka Street. 1889-93, architect N. Pozdeyev

The Tretyakov Gallery. In the foreground:
the monument to Pavel Tretyakov, founder
of the Gallery

The Vladimir Icon of Our Lady. ▶
Early 12th century, by an anonymous
Greek icon-painter

THE TRETYAKOV GALLERY

The now world-famous State Tretyakov Gallery began with two pictures by obscure Russian painters purchased in 1856 by Pavel Mikhailovich Tretyakov, the 24-year-old son of the owner of a linen factory. Thereafter, the Russian Maecenas continued to collect works by his gifted compatriots throughout his life. In 1892, he presented the following application to the Moscow municipal authorities: "Wishing to promote the establishment of useful institutions in this city which means so much to me, to contribute to the flourishing of the arts in Russia and, at the same time, to preserve my collection forever, I am hereby handing over to the Moscow

City Duma, as a gift, my entire picture gallery with all its works of art". By that time, Tretyakov's collection comprised 3,500 works.

The Tretyakov gallery was, for his contemporaries, a living history of Russian art. The best painters rallied around the collector, and helped him to enrich his gallery.

The Gallery building has an interesting history. At first, new premises were added to the house Tretyakov lived in. The need for such extra premises arose each time new major works were purchased, such as the Turkestan collection by Vereshchagin, paintings by I. Repin, V. Surikov. After the collection had been handed over to the city, the Gallery became a public building and had to be re-decorated accordingly. The well-known artist

St. Demetrius of Salonica,
12th-century mosaic

Works of ancient Russian art are among its most precious items. The collection of icons handed over to the Museum by the artist I.S. Ostroukhov has by now developed into a major display of medieval Russian painting.

Represented in it are various art schools including those of Moscow (featuring masterpieces by Andrei Rublyov), Rostov, Vladimir, Suzdal, Pskov. Icons which have come down to our times from Kievan Rus have a pride of place in the collection.

Vladimir Icon of Our Lady. The Vladimir Icon of Our Lady by a Greek master, brought to Kiev from Byzantium, dates back to the early 12th century. When it was installed in Vladimir in 1155, the icon was named for that town. Since the 14th century the icon has been housed in Moscow's Assumption Cathedral in the Kremlin. The Vladimir Icon of Our Lady is a great work of art which communicates to us, through the centuries, a strong message of tender motherly love.

St. Demetrius of Salonica. The mosaic picture St. Demetrius of Salonica, dating to the same century, conveys the epic spirit of Kievan Rus. Originally in the Mikhailovsky Zlatoverkhy Monastery in Kiev, it shows the folk hero who performed heroic deeds in the name of Russia, a warrior in rich attire and golden chain armour, with the strong face of a man who knows no fear.

Our Saviour Icon. Early 15th century.
By Andrei Rublyov

V. Vasnetsov undertook to make sketches of the front entrance to the gallery and of its façade and in 1902 the building was reconstructed to his sketches. Vasnetsov made skilful use of old Russian architectural motifs and as a result the Gallery building looks like a palace out of a fairy-tale.

After the Revolution, many artistic treasures were nationalized and handed over to the Gallery, which, as a result, had to be further enlarged. A .Shchusev, the well-known Soviet architect, reconstructed the Gallery and added extra exhibition space, but even these quarters became cramped as new pictures kept arriving. Recently, the Gallery was further expanded to include many monuments of architecture found in that old part of the city. Several new buildings have also been erected providing much larger exposition space. Today the Tretyakov Gallery owns over 57,000 works, a large proportion of which are kept in store-rooms for want of display space. Now these works will be put on a show.

ANDREI RUBLYOV. **Spas** (Saviour). The story behind this icon, a universally recognized masterpiece of world art, is unusual. Painted presumably at the beginning of the 15th century, the icon was rediscovered in 1918 in the ancient town of Zvenigorod near Moscow. Since the famous icon painter Rublyov had lived there for some time, experts reasoned that he must have left behind an icon or two. An expedition from Moscow was in for a disappointment, however. The iconostasis in the local church turned out to be relatively new — it dated back to the 17th century. The search for ancient icons continued in the annexes around the church. Not far from the Zvenigorod Cathedral, the experts happened upon a timber store and there, under a pile of firewood, they found three time-blackened boards coated with a layer of paint which had peeled off in places. A layer of dirt was wiped off to reveal icons which later came to be called Zvenigorod after the town where they were found. Those were the icons of the Saviour, the Archangel Michael and the Apostle Paul. Experts arrived at the conclusion that they could have been created only by Andrei Rublyov. The document confirming this was found later.

Since the early 14th century, the Christ of the Russian icon painters was full of light, kind and gentle. And Rublyov embodied just this in his Saviour, on an extremely high artistic level — the image of a loving god who brings consolation and hope.

F.S. ROKOTOV, D.G. LEVITSKY. Religious art predominated in Russia for seven centuries. In the period of Peter the Great's reform, portreture became the favourite genre which expressed a new humanitarian attitude to the individual. A fine psychologist capable of transferring to canvas the complicated world of human emotions, the famous F.S. Rokotov created a gallery of portraits of his contemporaries of the second half of the 18th century. In 1765, for instance, he painted a remarkable portrait of V.I. Maikov. Thanks to Rokotov, we can see today the face of the poet, a sybarite but also a clever man with a fine sense of humour.

In the portrait of young A.P. Struiskaya, the charm of her inspired face and the romantic mystery glowing in her eyes are set off by the blurred contours of her figure, which is in the shade.

The talented Russian portraitist D.G. Levitsky pictured people from various social strata of the late 18th — the early 19th centuries. One of his best works is the portrait of P.P. Demidov — the owner of numerous mines and metallurgical factories. He was highly intelligent, a masterful and strong-willed person.

V.I. SURIKOV. The famous painting **Boyarina Morozova** (1887) by V.I. Surikov affords the onlooker a profound insight into the human soul. The painting re-creates a dramatic page in Russian history — the division of the Russian Orthodox Church in the 17th century which led to the persecution of those who rejected Patriarch Nikon's innovations.

The artist depicted the moment when the manacled Boyarina Morozova, a fierce and frank adversary of Nikon's, is being sledged to a torture chamber along a Moscow street. A frantic fanatic, Morozova raises her hand high, with the first and second fingers pressed together in the seditious sign of dissent, as an overwhelmed crowd looks on. The faces around her run the whole gamut of feelings — fear, hatred, compassion, hope, malicious joy. The drama of the scene is set off by the intense colour scheme of the painting, by contrasts of white and almost black, by the overall atmosphere of nervous tension the artist conveys.

V.V. KANDINSKY. The Tretyakov Gallery collection gives one an idea of the turbulent development of new trends in the graphic arts of the early 20th century. Vasili Vasilyevich Kandinsky (1866-1944) was a pioneer of new art forms and had an enormous influence on world culture.

Kandinsky's paintings testify to his profound reflections and agonizing creative quests throughout his life as an artist, which lasted for about 50 years. Kandinsky took up painting rather late in life, at the age of 30. At first, he assimilated the experiences of various schools, styles and trends — German Jugendstyl and expressionism, Russian and European modernism. His own style took shape rather slowly and manifested itself in an outburst of individuality in the 1910s and 1920s.

The Tretyakov Gallery exposition features his mature works, such as **Improvisation No. 7** (1910) and **Vagueness** (1917). These paintings embody the artist's striving for a synthesis of the conscious and the subconscious, the intuitive and the rational.

Portrait of Ursula Mniszech. By Dmitri Levitsky

Boyarina Morozova. 1887. By Vasili Surikov

Seated Demon. 1890. By Mikhail Vrubel

Kandinsky emphasized the priority of spiritual content in art and made combinations of abstract shapes the chief means of expression.

In his numerous "improvisations" and "compositions" Kandinsky gave free rein to intuition and actively used his imagination in interpreting reality. The stories told by his paintings in terms of line and colour are composed of individual motifs, each self-contained, but all of them interacting with one another. Kandinsky's works can be described as "plays in colour", with blots and lines acting like living beings.

The artist pioneered many new laws governing the impact and perception of colours, lines, blots and shapes.

Composition No. 7. 1913. By Vasili Kandinsky

CHEKHOV HOUSE-MUSEUM

In the Sadovo-Kudrinskaya Street, near the Vosstania (formerly Kudrinskaya) Square, an unobtrusive mansion (No. 8) snuggles up to a huge multi-storeyed block of flats. A metal plaque on the mansion's door says: "Dr. A.P. Chekhov". The great Russian writer Anton Chekhov, whose plays run in almost all the theatres of the world and whose short stories and tales have been translated into almost all languages, rented the mansion before his departure for Sakhalin Island.

Chekhov lived in that house till 1890 when he decided to travel to the island, thousands of miles away from Moscow, which had long attracted him. The house was so small that the writer himself and his close friends referred to it, in jest, as a "chest of drawers". In it, Chekhov often played host to the writers V.A. Gilyarovsky, D.V. Grigorovich, V.G. Korolenko, the artist I.I. Levitan, the composer P.I. Tchaikovsky, the stage director V.I. Nemirovich-Danchenko, one of the founders of the Moscow Art Theatre.

Chekhov worked in his ground-floor study, the original furniture of which has largely survived intact. He created his tale **The Steppe,** the short story **Boredom,** the plays **Ivanov, Proposition, The Bear,** and other works there. Opened in 1954, the Museum draws hundreds of visitors.

◀ *Anton Chekhov House-Museum*

◀ *Fyodor Shaliapin Memorial Museum*

High-rise building of the Ministry of Foreign Affairs of the Russian Federation in Smolenskaya-Sennaya Square. 1948-52, architects V. Gelfreikh and M. Minkus

"The White House", premises of the Government of the Russian Federation

The Ukraine Hotel. 1950-57, architect A. Mordvinov

**Moscow State University
on Vorobyovy Hills**

**Church of the Holy Trinity
in Vorobyovo**

*Church of the Intercession
in Fili. Late 17th century*

*The Petrovsky Stopover Palace. Late 18th century,
architect M. Kazakov*

THE CHURCH OF THE INTERCESSION IN FILI

Late in the 17th century, Peter the Great presented the village of Fili to his uncle, L.K. Naryshkin. The vast area included in the Naryshkins' estate is now bespoken for by a park on the steep bank of the Moskva River and the Church of the Intercession in Fili, a magnificent example of 17th-century Russian architecture.

The church was built in 1693-1694 and is famous for the perfection of its forms and the richness of the white-stone ornamentation. It was one of the first works in the architectural style of the times known as the Naryshkin baroque. Inside are various remarkable works of Russian art: a nine-tiered carved gilt iconostasis, which rises right to the vaults, a carved choir loft, and a tent-roofed czar's pew executed by K. Zolotaryov, a noted 17th-century artist. The church was visited many times by Peter the Great and one of the paintings on the piers is believed to be his portrait as a young man.

After its restoration the church was converted into a concert hall where old Russian songs and instrumental music are performed.

THE PETROVSKY PALACE

With the transferral of the capital to St. Petersburg in the 18th century, the czar and his court left Moscow. Even so they paid frequent visits to the former capital and on these occasions the czars and czarinas would make a stopover in the village of Vsekhsvyatskoye. Wooden "journey palaces" had been built here where the royal family would rest before making ceremonial entry into Moscow. In 1776-1796, the Petrovsky Stopover Palace, to be used in place of the old wooden palaces, was built by the noted architect Matvei Kazakov on the site of the village of Petrovskoye.

Surrounded by brick fortress walls with towers, the palace combines the architectural techniques of neoclassicism with the vivid ornamental style of Old Russian building and the romantic features of Gothic. The interior decoration of the palace features the Louis XVI style.

In 1812 Napoleon, retreating from the Kremlin during the fire, spent several days at the palace.

The Triumphal Arch in Victory Square.
1827-34, architect Osip Bovet, sculptors
I. Vitali and I. Timofeyev

Poklonnaya Hill in the twilight

The St. George Church, a part
of the Victory Memorial Complex
on Poklonnaya Hill. 1995, architects
A. Polyansky and V. Budayev

THE NOVODEVICHY CONVENT

The Novodevichy Convent, which was also known in the days of old as the Convent of the Smolensk Icon of Our Lady, was founded by Grand Prince Vasili III in 1524 to commemorate the return of the city of Smolensk to Russia. The convent, built as a fortress in the bend of the Moskva River, became an important component of the capital's southern defence belt which consisted of the Donskoi Monastery, the Monastery of St. Daniel, the Monastery of St. Simeon, and other cloisters.

The fortress-convent played a part of some consequence in the struggle against the Tatar conquerors and the Polish invaders. In 1591, when the Crimean Khan Kazy Girei tried to cross the Moskva River and capture Moscow, the convent's cannon compelled the enemy to retreat. In 1612, the troops led by Dmitri Pozharsky defeated Hetman Chodkiewicz's detachments here.

In the 16th and 17th centuries the convent enjoyed a privileged position: it was here that women from the royal family and top-ranking boyar families took the veil. That is why its history is closely linked with the life of the Russian state in the 16th-early 18th centuries. Here czarina Irina, the wife of czar Fyodor Ioannovich and the sister of Boris Godunov, took the veil upon the czar's death in 1598. Here, that same year, Boris Godunov was proclaimed czar. Princess Sofia Alexeyevna, the sister of Peter the Great, was confined here for 15 years following an abortive attempt to deprive her brother of the throne.

The Novodevichy Convent itself is a unique 16th-17th century architectural ensemble. It is dominated by the huge five-domed Cathedral of the Smolensk Icon of Our Lady (1524-1525) which was modelled on the Cathedral of the Dormition in the Kremlin. In the early 17th century, during the reign of Boris Godunov, the walls of the cathedral were ornamented with frescoes representing historic episodes in the struggle for the formation of a centralised Russian state. In the 1680s, K. Mikhailov and O. Andreyev together with a number of other Russian master carvers created one of the finest ornamental works of the period — a multitiered gilt carved iconostasis, demonstrative of their exquisite taste and tremendous skill.

The Novodevichye Cemetery. The tomb of Fyodor Shaliapin, the great Russian bass singer

The Novodevichy Convent.
The Lopukhinskiye Chambers. 1680s

The iconostasis of the Cathedral of the Smolensk Icon ▶
of Our Lady. 17th century. Woodcarvers
K. Mikhailov and O. Andreyev

The floor of the cathedral is made of ornamental cast-iron plates. The other structures — the refectory, the gateway churches, the Irininskiye and Lopukhinskiye Chambers, and the cells — were also built in the 1680s. The decorative Moscow baroque style serves to harmonise the buildings with the abundance of white-stone ornamentation on the red-brick walls.

The convent's bell tower rivals the famous Bell Tower of Ivan the Great in the Kremlin in its beauty. Elegant and highly decorative it was erected in 1689-1690, and consists of six octagonal stepped tiers crowned with a gilt cupola. Each tier is surrounded by a balcony with a parapet supported by ornamental balusters.

Peter the Great, who was not particularly fond of cloisters, tried to use the Novodevichy Convent for practical purposes. On his orders, an orphanage for foundlings was set up at the convent and later on distinguished veteran soldiers were given food and shelter here.

In 1812, shortly before the retreat of the French from Moscow Napoleon ordered the convent to be blown up. Trenches were dug and filled with powder kegs. The convent was saved by the valiant Sister Sarra, the cloister's treasurer, who managed to extinguish the fuses connected to the kegs.

As soon as the convent was founded, a cemetery was opened on its grounds, which subsequently became a traditional burial place for the church dignitaries and feudal lords of Moscow and later on, in the 19th century, of the intelligentsia and merchants. The graves of quite a few prominent public and cultural figures famous in Russian history such as the Decembrists M. Muravyov-Apostol, A. Muravyov and S. Trubetskoi, the poet Denis Davydov who was a hero of the Patriotic War of 1812, the historian S. Solovyov, the writers A. Pisemsky, M. Zagoskin and I. Lazhechnikov, and others have been preserved in the burial grounds of the cloister.

In 1898, the so-called New Cemetery was established behind the south wall of the convent. Surrounded by a wall in 1898-1904, it became the most venerated cemetery in Moscow. Here lie the bodies of outstanding writers and poets such as N. Gogol, A. Chekhov, V. Bryusov and V. Mayakovsky, the artists V. Serov and I. Levitan, as well as famous actors, scientists and public figures. The body of N. Ogaryov was transferred here from Britain and that of F. Chaliapin, from France. The tombstones to be seen at the Novodevichye Cemetery include works by the celebrated Russian and Soviet sculptors N. Andreyev, M. Anikushin, V. Mukhina, and I. Shadr.

Church of Our Lady of Kazan. Mid-17th century;
opposite: Church of the Ascension. 16th century

KOLOMENSKOYE

The village of Kolomenskoye was first mentioned in the will of Ivan Kalita, but its history dates from the early 13th century when the inhabitants of Kolomna, seeking refuge from the Tatar-Mongol invaders led by Khan Batu, founded their settlement here. In the 15th-17th centuries it was an estate of the Moscow grand princes and then of the czars. Ivan the Terrible visited here and Peter the Great spent his childhood years on the estate. In 1606, during the so-called Time of Troubles, the troops of Ivan Bolotnikov, leader of the first Russian peasant war, pitched camp here, when they laid siege to the capital for five weeks in their attempt to take the city.

The tent-roofed stone Church of the Ascension, an outstanding masterpiece of world art, was built in Kolomenskoye in 1530-1532 by a great master whose name has long since been forgotten. Immediately after the church was built, a contemporary chronicler recorded the event in impassioned words, noting that no other church in Russia rivalled it in beauty.

In the 16th century the cylindrical candlelike Church and Belfry of St. George the Victorious — a slender two-tiered tower decorated with false arches and **kokoshniki** — was erected near the Church of the Ascension.

In the mid-17th century the stout five-domed Church of the Kazan Icon of Our Lady was built on a high basement

decorated with arches. Of particular interest among the other structures of that period are the Water Tower over the dam, which supplied the estate with water, the festive looking multi-tiered, tent-roofed Front Gate, which was the main entrance to the Royal Court, and the modest, single-storeyed Back Gate near which the princesses' **terems** stood. It was also then that the Kitchens, the Administrative and Regimental Chambers and the domestic church of the royal family were built.

Unfortunately, the wooden palace of czar Alexei Mikhailovich, a unique masterpiece of Russian architecture built in 1667-1668 by carpenter foreman S. Petrov and serf carpenter I. Mikhailov, has not survived. This beautiful palace consisted of a large number of buildings interconnected by passageways. Today the visitors to the museum can form an idea of what the palace looked like from the model skilfully executed by the woodcarver D. Smirnov in 1867, and also from old engravings.

A number of interesting examples of wooden structures have been brought to Kolomenskoye. They include a 17th-century mead brewery from the village of Preobrazhenskoye in the environs of Moscow, the tower from the Bratsk Stockade in Siberia (1652), the entrance tower from the Karelian Monastery of St. Nicholas at the mouth of the Northern Dvina River (1692), and

THE ST. DANIEL MONASTERY

Peter the Great's House from the Novodvinskaya Fortress near Arkhangelsk (1702).

The museum's display includes Russian tiles, cast-iron articles, carved wood and metal, and 17th-century icons. There are also permanent exhibitions dealing with the history of Kolomenskoye, palatial building, and the art of Russian blacksmiths, foundrymen and carpenters.

One other unique monument which has survived over the centuries is the ancient oak grove containing trees that are 600 to 800 years old.

This monastery was founded around 1282 by Prince Daniil Alexandrovich of Moscow in honour of his heavenly patron, St. Daniel the Stylite. Shortly before his death in 1303, Prince Daniil took monastic vows and on his demise he was buried here.

The St. Daniel Monastery, a monastery-fortress, played an important part in defending Moscow from attacks by the Crimean Tatars, in particular, in repulsing the raid of the troops led by Khan Kazy Girei in 1591. Early in December 1606, the peasant army of Ivan Bolotnikov fought a major battle against the

*The St. Daniel Monastery, now the residence
of the Patriarch of Moscow and All Russia.
13th century*

troops of czar Vasili Shuisky in front of the monastery, which
ended in the rout of the insurgents.

The surviving buildings, surrounded by mighty brick walls
with seven towers built in the 17th century, are a picturesque
sight. They include the Church of the Holy Fathers of the Seven
Ecumenical Councils (16th-18th centuries), the Church of St.
Daniel the Stylite over the cloister's Holy Gates (1732), the
cells of the brethren (1869), and the Trinity Church built in
1833 by architect Ye. Tyurin.

Today the St. Daniel Monastery has been turned over to the
Russian Orthodox Church and now it again functions as a
cloister.

THE ENVIRONS OF MOSCOW

The dense forests of age-old firs and thickest oaks, the pine and birch groves full of sun, the undulating plains criss-crossed with full-flowing rivers and murmuring creeks, the deep blue lakes and crystal-clear cool springs...This is the countryside around Moscow, "a land after my own heart", as a poet called it, the centre of Russia, with its towns, large and small, glowing golden in the night like strings of water lilies, with their villages scattered over the hills like mushrooms, and here and there, like a rare berry, an ancient estate, ages old, appearing suddenly in emerald-green glades.

The scenic beauty of central Russia, which charms the beholder with its unobtrusiveness, is in full harmony with these estates. In fact, the environs of Moscow are inconceivable without the onion-shaped domes of churches, large and small, without manor houses and parks, many of them pearls of palace and landscape architecture, without splendid historical and cultural monuments.

Most of the estates date back to the 18th-19th centuries. They owe their artistic merits to talented Russian architects, many of whom were serfs. Arkhangelskoye, Abramtsevo, Voronovo, Marfino, Ostafyevo, Vyazemy, Zvenigorod, Sukhanovo — such is a far from complete list of monuments of

estate architecture which have survived in the environs of Moscow to this day.

The architecture of the Russian estate has an age-old tradition behind it, and took shape in the epoch of serfdom. A typical estate comprises a manor house, service structures and a park. Although mostly of neoclassical architecture, each estate is unmistakably Russian.

Some of the estates are palatial, complete with porticoes, ornate façades, colonnades, galleries and belvederes; others are modest structures, with attic storeys and simple porches. Even most of the latter, however, are small masterpieces.

The interior decoration of the manor houses is distinguished by impeccable taste. Their ball-, guest-, dining- and bedrooms are decorated with fanciful stucco mouldings, tapestry, hand-painted ornaments, tiles, graceful furniture, paintings and sculptures, many of them by well-known masters, both Russian and European.

Landscape was an important consideration in selecting the place in which to build an estate. Much attention was paid to landscape architecture which also attained high artistic standards.

The estates in the environs of Moscow are not only of architectural and artistic value. Associated with them are the life and work of the outstanding Russian writers, artists, thinkers and public figures. The scenic beauty of the countryside around Moscow inspired artists, musicians, prose writers and poets in the creation of great works which have come to occupy a pride of place in national and world culture. In many estates, now turned into memorial museums, one can see the personal belongings of great men. The people and the state carefully preserve these relics, and add others as they are found. This is part of our heritage and we are proud of it. Anyone wishing to learn more about our national culture and history is offered a ready access to these treasures.

ABRAMTSEVO

The small estate of Abramtsevo, near Moscow, now a museum, has a special place in the history of Russian culture. Its cultural heritage rather than its architecture is why Abramtsevo attracts numerous tourists.

In 1843, the estate was purchased by S.T. Aksakov, the well-known writer and theatre critic. He fell in love with that out-of-town nook, with its cosy wooden mezzanine house, with its age-old park, the winding Vorya river, the ponds rich in fish, and the woods abounding in mushrooms. He called Abramtsevo "paradise on earth".

Aksakov's poetic descriptions of the Russian countryside were highly praised by Nekrasov, Turgenev, Chernyshevsky and Gorky.

The Abramtsevo Estate. Sergei Aksakov's House

Sergei Aksakov's study

Aksakov was a close friend of Gogol's. It was here, in Abramtsevo, that Gogol recited the first chapters of his "Dead Souls". Aksakov also played host to the famous actor M. Shchepkin and to many representatives of the progressive Russian intelligentsia — V. Belinsky, A. Herzen, M. Bakunin, S. Granovsky, A. Koltsov, T. Shevchenko who often discussed literary, philosophical and socio-political problems with Aksakov, as well as the future of the Russian people, whom all of them wanted to see prosperous and happy. After Aksakov's death in 1859, the estate temporarily fell into a slumber.

In 1870, Abramtsevo came back to life when the deserted estate was purchased by Savva Mamontov, a wealthy industrialist, a patron of literature and art, a man of progressive views. Active, witty and endowed with excellent artistic taste, he had a nose for talent, helping and supporting artists in every way. In particular, he patronized Chaliapin, Vasnetsov and other artists now well-known far outside our country.

In Mamontov's house, with its warm and friendly atmosphere, they formed an artistic circle which included the famous painters I. Repin, V. Polenov, the brothers V. and A. Vasnetsov, V. Serov, K. Korovin, M. Nesterov, M. Vrubel, V. Surikov. In Abramtsevo, Repin created his **Seeing Off a Recruit** and worked on sketches for his celebrated picture **A Religious Procession in Kursk Gubernia.** At a boisterous party, Repin conceived of his **Zaporozhye Cossacks** — and got down to work rightaway. The very landscapes around Abramtsevo inspired artists, who created many of their masterpieces there — **Alyonushka** (V. Vasnetsov), **The River Vorya** (Polenov), **A Vision of Young Varfolomei** (Nesterov), **A Girl With Peaches** (Serov). Incidentally, Mamontov's son Andrei sat for Vasnetsov when the latter painted Alyosha Popovich, one of his **Russian Warriors.**

Mamontov opened a carpentry shop in Abramtsevo in which folk craftsmen made decorated furniture and the children of the local peasants learned carpentry. Later, a pottery was set up and the workers tried to find out how ancient Russian tiles had been made. Vrubel worked in the pottery shop with great inspiration. The vases, dishes, mantelpieces and majolica figurines he made graced the interior of the estate.

The Red Drawing Room in the house

Mizgir. Majolica, 1899-1900.
By Mikhail Vrubel

The artists also designed theatricals which were a great success in Abramtsevo. Mamontov established the private Russia Opera Company which fostered the talents of Borodin, Mussorgsky, Rimsky-Korsakov.

In every room of the house there are relics associated with the names of the men of genius who once visited the estate: household articles, paintings, sketches for stage scenery designs, sculpture, various hand-made objects.

A small structure in old-Russian style with carved lintels, banisters and plinths will certainly catch your eye. This is a bath-house designed by the architect I. Petrov, better known under the pseudonym Ropet. In the middle of the park are ancient stone idols brought in by S. Mamontov. V. Vasnetsov built a fairy-tale "House on Hen Legs" for Mamontov's children and the family burial vault is next to the church, designed by V. Vasnetsov and V. Polenov.

The Abramtsevo State Historical, Art and Literary Preserve-Museum is a worthy monument to great men of Russian culture.

TSARITSINO

The Tsaritsino estate, built at the end of the 18th century, is now situated between the Proletarsky Prospekt and Kashirskoye Shosse, within city limits. At the beginning of the 18th century the estate, then called Chornaya Gryaz, belonged to the father of A. Kantemir, the well-known Russian satirical poet, philosopher and diplomat. In 1775, it was purchased by Catherine II who made it her country residence — "in order to live near Moscow like an ordinary member of the landed gentry", she explained. She commissioned the well-known Russian architect V. Bazhenov to design the residence.

It took him about a decade to create a unique group of buildings which harmonized with the surrounding scenery and embodied the architect's original ideas. Bazhenov used not only elements of traditional Russian architecture, but those of medieval Gothic as well. The resultant style came to be known as pseudo-Gothic. The fanciful park gates, the white-stone openwork structures and Gothic archways are typical of this style. Lacy white-stone ornaments decorated the large and small red-brick palace buildings.

The palaces, pavilions, archways and bridges, galleries and artificial ruins fitted in amazingly well with the undulating wooded landscape, ravines and ponds. This fusion of art and nature was aptly described by a poet as: "Architecture which sets off nature's own beauty to the best advantage".

In 1786, Catherine II, displeased with the main palace, ordered the whole structure to be torn down.

The well-known Russian architect M. Kazakov, commissioned to build a new palace, largely preserved the concept of his famous predecessor but also threw in some ideas of his own for good measure. The war with Turkey, which all but drained the public purse, prevented him from completing the project. The half-finished Main Palace, the Bread House connected with it by means of a gallery, the Opera House, the Cavaliers' Block, the Grape and Mermaid Gates, a string of ponds with fanciful bridges have survived to this day.

Tsaritsino remains a masterpiece of Russian neoclassicism, a remarkable monument to the talent of the great Russian architects. Restoration work is in progress there now.

BOLSHIYE VYAZYOMY

The Bolshiye Vyazyomy estate is of historical as well as architectural interest. Suffice it to say, that it was Boris Godunov's country residence at the end of the 16th century. Judging by chronicles, the Trinity church (renamed Transfiguration at the end of the 17th century) and a stone dam near the pond were under construction there in the reign of czar Fyodor Ioannovich (i.e., before the year 1598).

This church ranks among the outstanding monuments of 16th-century Russian architecture. With its then traditional five domes and high ground floor, it merges with the symmetrical side annexes on the altar side into a single whole. Thanks to such an unusual fusion, the altar part is impressively vast. Plans of this type became widespread at the end of the 16th century.

The church walls consist of white stone slabs all the way up to the top, which is brickwork. Some architects regard the church as an imitation of the Moscow Kremlin's Archangel Cathedral. The lavish decoration of the church with carved-stone elements make it a prototype of sorts for the ornate churches of the 17th century.

The Trinity church was frescoed right after its completion, i.e. at the turn of the 17th century. When it was refurbished a century ago some of the frescoes were lost. In the process of restoration, started over thirty years ago, the more recent layers of plaster were removed to reveal the initial frescoes — Sarah in Doubt and Prophecy to Abraham.

On the whole, the frescoes of the 16th-century church are much like those of the Smolensky Cathedral in Moscow's Novodevichy Convent, a monument of the so-called "Godunov school of painting". Most of them show the deeds of the Trinity for which the church had been initially named. The tombstone commemorating Prince B.V. Golitsyn who died in action at Borodino used to be in the northern annex (later it was transferred to the Donskoi Monastery).

A three-span belfry stands next to the church on a ground-floor. The historical events related to the estate Bolshiye Vyazyomy are as follows. In 1606, Marina Mniszech, the bride of the claimant to the Russian throne who called himself "Dmitry I",

Tsaritsyno. The Grape Gate.
18th century,
architect Vasili Bazhenov

Bolshiye Vyazyomy Estate. Golitsyn's manor-house.
Late 18th century

The Trinity Church (the Transfiguration).
16th century

stopped over there on her way to Moscow. In 1611, peace talks were held there with the Polish Hetman J. Sapiega. During the Patriotic War of 1812, Kutuzov stopped over there, and later Napoleon spent the night in the estate before marching into Moscow.

At the end of the 17th century, Peter I presented Bolshiye Vyazyomy to the Golitsyn family. The Pushkins used to visit the place taking their son, the future great poet, along (he was a mere child then). The poet's junior brother, Nikolai, is buried in the cemetery of the Trinity church, at its eastern wall. The tombstone — a small grey limestone column — has survived. The Golitsyn family owned the estate right until the October Revolution. Their two-storey brick manor house, built at the end of the 18th century, still stands. The influence of neoclassical French architecture is clearly evident. The magnificent park laid out in front of the house at about the same time has survived, in part.

There is reason to believe that in his tragedy **Boris Godunov** Pushkin drew upon the old legend he had heard in Bolshiye Vyazyomy about the Time of Troubles, "Dmitry I", Marina Mniszech and czar Boris.

Sukhanovo Estate. The manor-house.
Late 18th century

A Girl with a Broken Jug statue
in Sukhanovo park

SUKHANOVO

The Sukhanovo estate lies three kilometres from the Rastorguyev station on the Paveletskaya railway. Its architecture took final shape at the end of the 18th and at the beginning of the 19th century when the princely family of Volkonsky owned it. The estate was built by the best architects of the times. Although many of the structures have lost their original appearance, and some lie in ruins Sukhanovo remains a remarkable monument of Russian architecture and landscaping.

Sukhanovo consists of three parts: the manor house proper with its church, service structure, and the Volkonsky family mausoleum. The manor with its outbuildings, two guest houses, some service structures, a reconstructed and refurbished mausoleum, the park with its ponds, fanciful bridges and pergolas set up in picturesque places are in a good state of preservation.

The central manor house, built at the end of the 18th century, is basically neoclassical even though it was restored at the beginning of the new century and became more of a palace of somewhat eclectic and ornate style.

The façade, overlooking the front yard, is decorated with a colonnaded rotunda. On the park side, the house has a six-

Sukhanovo Estate. Office building

The mausoleum of the Volkonsky princes. 1813

column portico with an attic storey. The outbuildings on both sides communicate with it by means of colonnaded galleries. After 1917, the house burned down. In the post-war years, the Volkonsky manor house was fully restored under the direction of the architect V.D. Kokorin.

The mausoleum (burial vault) of the Princes Volkonsky, built in 1813 in the Empire style, is of special interest. It was supposedly designed by the well-known architects D.I. Gilardi and A.G. Grigoryev. Originally, it was a rotunda with symmetrical wings attached to it on either side and with a semi-circular colonnade. The reconstruction of 1934 as projected by the architect N.V. Vinogradov detracted from the harmony of the building, but not from its magnificence. The splendid interior of the rotunda, the harmonious original proportions of the round hall, the hand-painted ornament of the cupola remained intact. Near the mausoleum is a statue of **A Girl With a Broken Jug** by an unknown sculptor. Visitors can admire the park (i.e. what is left of it) with its cascade of terraced ponds.

Sukhanovo ranks high among the early-19th-century monuments of architecture. It is often described, with good reason, as a pearl among the former estates of the nobility in Moscow's environs.

ARKHANGELSKOYE

Arkhangelskoye, a small village on the precipitous bank of the Moskva river, was first mentioned in a chronicle in the 16th century. The estate as such was built in the second half of the 17th century under Boyar Ya.N. Odoyevsky. A manor house and the church of Archangel Michael were built there; the external appearance of the latter changed many times, but it now looks as it once did thanks to the restoration carried out at the end of the 1960s.

In 1703 Arkhangelskoye went to Prince D.M. Golitsyn, a prominent statesman, an associate of Peter I. A new manor house was built there, and a regular, or "French", park laid out. The estate, originally designed by the architect Charles des Guerne, took final shape under Prince N.B. Yusupov, grandee of Catherine II, well-known collector and connoisseur of the arts. A diplomat who had travelled far and wide in Europe, he met Rousseau, Voltaire and Beaumarchais and held views considered progressive for his times. It was he who had the exterior and interior decoration of the palace and park structures completed and joined into a single whole.

Prince Yusupov moved his rich art collections, which included a picture gallery regarded as one of Russia's best, to Arkhangelskoye. The gallery comprised over 500 works by leading European masters. In addition, Yusupov had the park decorated with sculptures, brought in rare pieces of furniture and beautiful china- and bronzeware.

A fire severely damaged the palace interior. However, the French artists Nicolas de Courteille, Columbie and Runge, as well as serf craftsmen, redecorated the interiors and restored the ornamentation. These interiors in a late neoclassical style have on the whole survived.

In the centre of the Palace there is the oval hall intended for ball parties and receptions. The cupola, decorated by Nicolas de Courteille, shows Cupid and Psyche soaring in clouds. In the Imperial Hall next to it, the walls are hung with paintings of Russian monarchs — Paul I (by S.S. Shekhukin) and Alexander I with his retinue (by the French painters Swebach and Riesener).

On the whole, paintings and sculptures by Western European masters predominate among the works of art found in the palace. They are, to name but a few, a marble bust of Paris by the well-known Italian sculptor Antonio Canova (the late 18th century); the marble sculpture **A Warrior Putting On His Armour** by the German sculptore Emil Wolff (the 19th century), **Melancholic** and **Choleric,** two male figures by an unknown Western European sculptor. Two corner rooms of the palace were decorated by the 18th-century French painter Hubert Robert, who did an especially good job of the antique hall featuring original sculptures of the first-third centuries A.D.

Although it is hard to enumerate all the outstanding masters whose works are represented in the palace, one cannot possibly fail to mention the French painters François Boucher and Elizabeth Vigee-Lebrun, the Spanish painter Francisco Romas, the brilliant Italian master Giovanni Battista Tiepolo, the Frenchmen Gabriel François Doyen and Jean Tassel (the 17th century). **The Sacrifice of Iphigeneia** is the only work by this outstanding master to be found in our country. The collection of Dutch and Flemish masters, built up by Yusupov, is unique. The names of Van Dyck and Abraham van Diepenbeeck speak for themselves.

A papier-mâché figure of Jean-Jacques Rousseau, seated in an armchair, testifies to the estate owner's free thought. Yusupov kept it in his library.

The unique park is certainly one of the greatest attractions of Arkhangelskoye. Its perfect geometrical composition and inimicable beauty place it among the best examples of Russian landscape architecture of the turn of the 19th century. The park forms a semi-circle, leaving the façade of the palace open to view. The upper, or minor, terrace of the park directly adjoins the palace. The central alley divides it into two symmetrical parterres, with other lanes running parallel. The upper terrace is decorated with tapered pillars crowned with sculptured antique heads, and the sculptured group Hercules and Anteus — a copy of the Roman original.

The lower terrace communicates with the upper by means of a stairway decorated with sculptures. A small fountain is flanked by two identical statues of Cupid bending his bow. The bottom terrace gradually expands into a large parterre measuring 240 by 70 metres, decorated with more sculptures, pergolas, balustrades, pavilions, and stylized ruins. Scattered all over the park, they add greatly to its glory. The Caprice pavilion, the Tea House, the Catherine Temple pergola with a bronze figure of Themis are particularly expressive.

On the next pages: General View ▶
of Arkhangelskoye Palace

Arkhangelskoye Estate. The entrance
gate. 18th century

Arkhangelskoye Estate. The study

A Girl Apprehended in Bathing. 18th century.
By François Boucher

A Landscape. 17th century. By Claude Lorrain

There were many celebrities among the guests of Arkhangelskoye. The great Russian poet Alexander Pushkin visited it on more than one occasion. A bronze bust of the poet was installed on one of the alleys, among those of antique gods and philosophers, to commemorate his visits. This alley, which runs near the palace, is known as Pushkinskaya. Next to the Pushkin monument is the bronze figure of a young man holding a torch with its flame dying down. This sculpture by the German master Carl-Georg Barth is called **Sorrow.**

The magnificent harmony and beauty of its palace and park make Arkhangelskoye a major tourist attraction.

An old clock

The Arakcheyev tea-set

◀Arkhangelskoye Estate. The Cupid and Psyche plafond in the Oval Room. 18th century. By Nicholas de Courteille

Ostankino Estate of Count Nikolai Sheremetev. 18th century

On the next pages: Ostankino Palace. The Italian Hall

OSTANKINO

The Ostankino Estate, one of the best-known 18th-century Moscow suburban estates (today it is well within the limits of the city), is an outstanding masterpiece of Russian neoclassicism. This appraisal is corroborated, among other things, by the enthusiastic description of the Ostankino Palace, furnished by the Englishman, Paget, where he described it as "exceeding everything in grandeur and magnificence that the most fertile imagination and the boldest artistic fantasy could ever conceive of". The great French writer Stendhal was no less enthusiastic about his visit to Ostankino. The idea of building the palace-theatre was conceived by Count Nikolai Sheremetev,

one of the wealthiest and most influential men of his day. He launched the construction in 1791, commissioning the architect Francesco Camporesi and his own serf architects Pavel Argunov, Alexei Mironov and Grigori Dikushin to do the job. It was, above all, through their efforts that the palace astonished the contemporaries with its splendour. Though built of wood, the plaster finish gives the impression of stone. The U-shaped palace consists of a central building and two wing pavilions connected to it by single-storeyed galleries. The grandeur of the façade is emphasized by the solemn portico over the entrance above which rises an airy dome. The

Ostankino Palace. The Blue Hall

*Portrait of Count Nikolai Sheremetev.
By Nikolai Argunov*

ten-column loggia-portico along the entire second floor of the garden façade enhances the stylistic unity of the building. The architects certainly succeeded in turning the palace into a perfect work of art.

The main hall, called the Theatre Hall, is in the central building of the palace. The performances staged here attracted many eminent theatre-lovers. Sheremetev's theatre company consisted of 200 talented serf actors, singers, dancers and musicians. The stars of the stage were the first dancer Tatiana Shlykova-Granatova and the singer Praskovya Kovalyova-Zhemchugova (the latter subsequently became the wife of Count Sheremetev). Both of them were enfranchised.

The Ostankino Theatre was unique in that the technical equipment used to produce various stage effects was indeed remarkable for the times. The floors, for instance, could be raised and lowered quickly and the auditorium together with the stage be transformed into a ballroom and vice versa.

The palace theatre

Portrait of Praskovya Kovalyova-Zhemchugova, a singer. By an anonymous artist

The palace with its pavilions had several ceremonial halls such as the Egyptian Hall used for concerts and banquets, the Italian Hall used for receptions, and also the Picture Gallery, the Blue Hall, and the Purple Drawing-Room. Each room has its own distinctive decor, executed with great artistic mastery. All the rooms are decorated with gilt carving, which is particularly characteristic of the Italian Pavilion where the walls are adorned with gilt carved panels.

The patterned parquet floors in the halls are also genuine works of art. Their fanciful patterns are made up of rare types of wood such as palm, rosewood, walnut, abony, redwood, karelian birch, and others.

The Picture Gallery of the Ostankino Palace boasts an interesting collection in which almost all the West European schools of painting are represented. There are also a number of portraits of serf actors and actresses, as well as local inhabitants, produced by the serf artists Ivan Argunov and Nikolai Argunov (father and son).

Kuskovo Estate. The wooden palace. 18th century, architect K. Blank

KUSKOVO

It is hard to imagine what prompted the Sheremetevs to choose this "God-forsaken" corner as the site of their future estate, Kuskovo. Indeed, the marshy flatland with its sparse woods could hardly serve as a source of inspiration for an architect, a decorator or an artist. And it certainly did not seem to be the right place for creating this splendid palatial estate which came to be known among contemporaries as the Moscow Versailles. And yet the ingenuity and great artistic taste of its builders enabled them to achieve the impossible. The Russian serf architects Fyodor Argunov, Alexei Mironov and Grigori Dikushin, with the participation of Karl Blank, created a true work of art.

Two ramps lead up to the entrance with its colonnaded portico. It is well worth while to pause before entering the building and survey the beautiful landscape that stretches out around the villa — the smooth expanse of the lake, the canal that runs from its far shore into the woods and the avenue beyond that leads to the tent-roofed Church of the Dormition of Our Lady in Veshnyaki. This principle of building a perspective architectural ensemble is characteristic of the whole of Kuskovo with its main palace, conservatory, Dutch and Italian houses, the Hermitage, and the Grotto.

A similar perspective is to be seen in the enfilade of palace rooms. After the vestibule, decorated with imitation marble and adorned with pilasters and grisaille painting, come the

The Grotto and the Dutch House.
Architect F. Argunov

drawing-rooms, the dining-room, and the private apartments of the palace owners. Compared with the vestibule, they are not very large and are less formal. The elegant furniture, the bookcases lining the walls, the wallpaper in a variety of warm colours, the Gobelin tapestries, the paintings, engravings and pieces of sculpture create a cosy and harmonious atmosphere. One by one, the rooms grow smaller and smaller, seemingly coming to a dead end, a "snuff-box room"... And then all of a sudden, the artist's wonderful fantasy explodes in a vast and light ballroom. The sparkling crystal chandeliers enhance the festive beauty of the room and lift one's spirits as soft music seems to be wafted in the air.

The wide windows of the ballroom open onto the great carpet of the lawn and the stone conservatory with a fanciful turret in the centre. There was once a concert hall under the spherical hexagonal dome of the conservatory which was noted for exotic tropical plants and fruits: it produced pineapples, peaches, apricots, oranges, and, even, coffee beans. The conservatory also supplied the park with tree saplings and flower seedlings. Near the pond stands the Dutch House which introduces the visitor to the architecture and art of 18th-century Holland. Even its kitchen is fitted out with a Dutch oven. The Italian House with a miniature garden, a fountain, statues, and a small pond serves the same purpose.

The buildings of the complex and, in particular, the main

palace, contain various paintings by European masters. They serve, in the main, as decorations for the palace interiors. It is worth while, however, to pay special attention to the collection of still lifes by Russian artists of the 1730s and 1740s, above all, those by G. Teplov, to be seen in the Sofa Room. One of Teplov's paintings shows a bookshelf containing books, a little bell and a bottle, with a parrot perching beside it and a picture of a sailboat underneath, below which is a chronometer, a comb, and a sealed envelope. This unexpected selection of objects seems to be ready to fall apart any moment, yet some unknown force continues to hold them together — a mystery which is over two centuries old.

Speaking about Kuskovo's collections, the Museum of Porcelain, subsequently renamed the State Museum of Ceramics, should be mentioned. It boasts unique specimens of Russian, Chinese, German, French, English and Danish porcelain, antique ceramics, faience, majolica, glass, and crystal.

NOVY IERUSALIM

This unique historical and architectural monument, whose name means New Jerusalem, is located not far from the town of Istra in the environs of Moscow. In the 17th century, Patriarch Nikon, who is known in history for his radical church reforms, decided to glorify the power and might of the Russian Orthodox Church by building a new house of worship. According to his ambitious plan, the new cathedral on the bank of the Istra River was to be a repetition of the Church of the Resurrection of Christ in Jerusalem. The church — a magnificent imaginative edifice was actually built. Russian master builders, however, after repeating the layout, topography and dimensions of the Jerusalem church, introduced vivid national features into

Kuskovo Estate. Park sculpture

Farmstead in Novy Ierusalim

Novy Ierusalim. The cathedral. 18th century

The wooden Church of the Epiphany

their design. Subsequently, these features were further developed in the Russian baroque style.

For example, for the first time ever they used tiles for decorating the building. In beauty and expressiveness they were on a par with the marble ornamentation of the Church of the Resurrection of Christ in Jerusalem. Particularly impressive were the three-tiered tiled iconostases of the cathedral's side chapels.

The buildings enclosed within the monastery's stone fortress walls with tent-roofed towers included the cathedral, the Patriarch's skete, the refectory, and the infirmary. Over the main entrance to the monastery was built the gate Church of the Entry into Jerusalem.

Unfortunately, the cathedral built by Nikon did not last long. Its majestic dome, the biggest in Russian church architecture of the period, collapsed and the destruction was completed by a fire. Soon a new cathedral was built in its place on the order of Empress Elizabeth Petrovna. It had the appearance of a splendid palace in the baroque style lavishly ornamented both inside and out.

Great material and cultural treasures found their way into the Novy Ierusalim Monastery, whose feudal possessions included large fisheries and saltworks. The finest craftsmen, artists and architects, among them Rastrelli, Blank, Kazakov, and Voronikhin, had a hand in polishing this architectural gem. The history of the monastery is linked with the names of Mikhail Lermontov, Alexander Herzen and Anton Chekhov. The great Russian military leader Alexander Suvorov lies buried here.

Today the architectural ensemble of the Novy Ierusalim Monastery houses a history and art museum.

Marfino Estate. Bridge over the pond and jetty sculptures

MARFINO

The history of the Marfino Estate commenced in 1585. It was built by V.Ya. Shchelkalov, an eminent statesman of the period, and subsequently it changed hands many times. Among its owners were Prince B.A. Golitsyn, the tutor of Peter the Great, P.S. Saltykov, Commander-in-Chief of the Moscow garrison, Count Orlov, and Count Panin.

The estate was rebuilt several times. Under Golitsyn, characteristic features of the Moscow baroque appeared. Later on, neoclassicism characterized the buildings. The surviving manor house with wings, the stable, the coach-house, and the oldest structure on the estate, the Church of the Nativity, near which the serf architect V. Belozerov, who built Golitsyn's estate, lies buried, are all witnesses of different historical events and reflect different architectural trends. The estate, however, does not appear to be eclectic. Perhaps, the secret of the ensemble's harmony lies in the picturesque setting with the scenery typical of Central Russia. The park of the estate is a fine example. The hills, trees, pond, summerhouses and pavilions and the wide terraced stone staircase are all harmoniously blended in this man-made park. The double-arched bridge across the pond, which served as the main entrance to the estate, lends it special charm all its own. Built of red bricks and decorated with white stucco moulding, it lies at the foot of Marfino like a piece of airy lace.

VALUYEVO

Compared with numerous other suburban manors, Valuyevo is an estate of a rather moderate size. It was built in the early 18th century by A.I. Musin-Pushkin, a well-known archeologist and bibliophile, who voluntarily or not created a classical sample of Moscow suburban architecture, incorporating every element characteristic of such a complex.

The two-storeyed manor house is connected to its two side wings by colonnaded galleries. The main courtyard is surrounded by service buildings with their own small yards. Round the manor house is a park with grottoes and a cascade of ponds. A wide avenue leads to the main courtyard. The entire layout is elegant, compact, beautiful and very comfortable by the yardsticks of the period.

The whole ensemble is built in the same style, late neoclassicism, and the façade of each of its buildings, be it the manor house, the stockyard or the stable, is ornamented with a monumental portico. There is an air of solidity, dignity and sedateness — traits which also apparently characterized the owner of the estate, whose research work brought fame to the name of Musin-Pushkin: he discovered a hand-written copy of **The Lay of Igor's Host** and thus presented Russia with a unique monument of Old Russian literature.

Valuyevo Estate. Water tower and a hunting lodge

Zagorsk (now Sergiyev Posad); top:
the Cathedral of the Dormition
(16th cent.); opposite: a panoramic view
of the Trinity-St. Sergy Lavra

ZAGORSK

Located in the town of Zagorsk 70 kilometres to the northwest of Moscow is the famous Trinity-St. Sergy Lavra, the biggest Russian monastery founded in the mid-14th century by Sergy of Radonezh. Hegumen Sergy was the first among those clergymen who openly supported the resistance against the Tatar invaders. It was he who gave his blessing to Moscow Grand

Prince Dmitri Donskoi, who took command of the joint Russian armies, on the eve of the historic Battle on Kulikovo Field. The people have not forgotten the moral feat of Sergy of Radonezh, paying him a tribute of admiration during his lifetime and venerating his memory upon his death. The monastery he founded became a kind of ideological centre of work for the unity of the Russian land, an inspiration for Russian patriotism, and a symbol of national independence.

Over its long history, a great number of beautiful icons, jewellery pieces, embroideries, and other superb works of art have been donated to the Trinity-St. Sergy Lavra. Today these fine masterpieces are kept at the Zagorsk History and Art Museum-Reserve where the exhibition acquaints the visitor with the history of the development of Russian art from the 15th century on.

The picturesque ensemble of the monastery itself, comprising over 50 buildings and structures, is a true gem of Russian architecture.

The Trinity-St. Sergy Lavra houses the Moscow Theological Academy and Seminary.

The All-Russia Exhibition Centre (former the USSR Economic Achievements Exhibition).
View of the Central part with
the Friendship of Peoples Fountain

THE USSR ECONOMIC ACHIEVEMENTS EXHIBITION

Back in 1939, a permanent All-Union Agricultural Exhibition was set up in Moscow. On its grounds, covering an area of more than 140 hectares, over 250 buildings (pavilions, conservatories, etc.) were erected, numerous fruit-bearing and decorative trees were planted and flower gardens were laid out. Since 1959, the USSR Economic Achievements Exhibition has been functioning here in Ostankino. Operating all the year round, it gives the visitor a comprehensive picture of the latest achievements of Soviet industry, agriculture, culture, and health care. The Exhibition grounds are also a venue of numerous international exhibitions.
The well-cared-for green zone of the Exhibition has become a favourite recreation haunt of the Muscovites.